Quit smoking for good

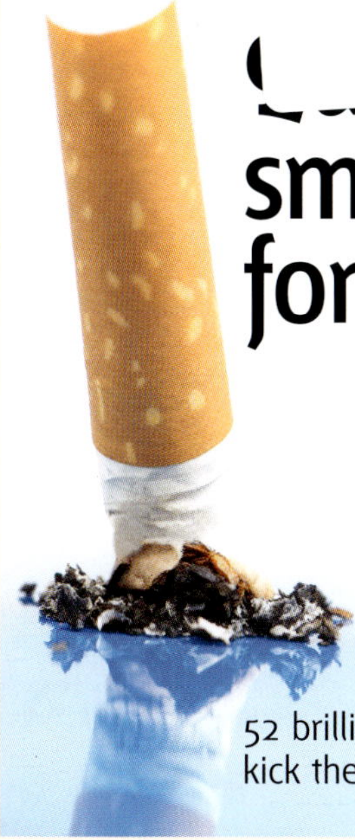

52 brilliant little ideas to kick the habit

Clive Hopwood and Peter Cross

CAREFUL NOW

Follow the tips in this book and you could soon be well on your way to a smoke-free life. Please also remember to consult your GP for help and advice on quitting, especially if you're planning on making changes to your diet or exercise routine. Remember that this is a book to help you on your journey, not a magic wand – kicking the habit is going to take effort and we can't be there to stub out every cigarette for you. You can do it if you put your mind to it – good luck!

Copyright © The Infinite Ideas Company Ltd, 2007

The right of Clive Hopwood and Peter Cross to be identified as the authors of this book has been asserted in accordance with the Copyright, Designs and Patents Act 1988.

First published in 2007 by
The Infinite Ideas Company Limited
36 St Giles
Oxford, OX1 3LD
United Kingdom
www.infideas.com

All rights reserved. Except for the quotation of small passages for the purposes of criticism or review, no part of this publication may be reproduced, stored in a retrieval system or transmitted in any form or by any means, electronic, mechanical, photocopying, recording, scanning or otherwise, except under the terms of the Copyright, Designs and Patents Act 1988 or under the terms of a licence issued by the Copyright Licensing Agency Ltd, 90 Tottenham Court Road, London W1T 4LP, UK, without the permission in writing of the publisher. Requests to the publisher should be addressed to the Permissions Department, Infinite Ideas Limited, 36 St Giles, Oxford, OX1 3LD, UK, or faxed to +44 (0)1865 514777.

A CIP catalogue record for this book is available from the British Library
ISBN 978-1-905940-30-1

Brand and product names are trademarks or registered trademarks of their respective owners.

Designed and typeset by Baseline Arts Ltd, Oxford

Southend-on-Sea Borough Libraries

Brilliant ideas

Introduction 11

1. Hail the weed 13
Feel free to smoke while you read this book. We should celebrate why smoking lights us up.

2. Tobacco tribe 15
Persecuted smokers take comfort in numbers so giving up without alienating your smoker chums takes planning.

3. Know your foe 17
What kind of smoker are you? Knowing the scale of your problem helps you form a plan of action to beat the habit.

4. Curse Raleigh 19
Learn from the past and change your future. Look at the centuries of mistakes and stupidity of our smoking ancestors.

5. The seven stages 21
Other smokers have given up before you. Follow the phases most of them went through.

6. Imagine 23
Creating morbid pictures in your mind's eye can be effective in helping to put you off smoking.

7. The fat issue 25
Let's think about why some, though not all, smokers gain weight after giving up and what can be done to avoid it.

8. Superkings? 27
Almost all smokers wish they'd never started, so how come so many of us fall into the deadly trap?

9. Smoking gun 31
The ill effects of smoking sneak up on us. Don't ignore them or make excuses.

10. **Poison cocktail** 33
Line up for your deadly dose of poisons and see just what goes inside your body every time you light up.

11. **Older sooner** 35
Seeing the impact smoking has on your face and body should give you the needed push.

12. **Tobacco giants** 37
Someone out there is getting very rich – at your expense – selling a deadly drug. Let's find out who.

13. **Spot the pitch** 39
Knowing how tobacco is marketed might not help you give up, but at least you'll know what you're up against.

14. **How much?!** 41
You pay through the nose for your habit. Look at the hidden costs of smoking and you're even worse off.

15. **Time to quit** 43
Waiting until you feel completely committed to giving up is as futile as herding cats.

16. **Diversion ahead** 45
Willpower alone may not be enough. Discovering ploys to distract yourself from cravings can prevent a relapse.

17. **Suck it and see** 47
Help is at hand. Nicotine replacement therapy (NRT) is available at the chemist's or on prescription.

18. **Cold turkey** 49
A short, sharp shock or a phased withdrawal? A case can be made either way.

19. **Super drugs** 53
Discover a drug that effectively curbs cravings and reduces withdrawals.

20. **Smoke screen** 55
Beating nicotine reliance is the easy bit. Defeating the psychological web of addiction beneath is a tougher task.

21. **Air equals life** 57
Simple fact: without air we die. So, how can anyone in their right mind choose to screw up their airways?

Brilliant ideas

22. The alternatives 59
'New age' treatments are worth a try. Most have been around far longer than cigarettes and draw on ancient wisdom.

23. First of the day 61
You want it simple? This is it: never smoke your first cigarette of the day again and you've stopped for ever.

24. Climb the ladder 63
Some people stop but start again over years. Even when they don't smoke, at heart they still feel like smokers.

25. Words on paper 67
Keeping a record of your struggle to quit will help you stay on track and give you something to be proud of.

26. Beat the weed 69
Familiar behaviour is full of triggers for the smoking reflex. Change the patterns and flummox the Tobacco Demon.

27. Feel lucky? 71
We know smoking's a risky business, but just how does it compare with other life-threatening activities?

28. Indiscriminate 73
Prince or pauper, millionaire or milkman – tobacco ruthlessly slays any of its users.

29. Smell of success 75
When quitting seems impossible, it's time to remind yourself that there are myriad smokers who *have* stopped.

30. Phone a friend 77
Finding the right person to help you quit could be the difference between success and failure.

31. Shared air 79
There are almost always people around you when you smoke. What are you doing to them?

32. Team player 83
If you've not got the willpower to go it alone, joining a group could give you the extra resolve.

33. I want it now 85
Ever wondered why sound health and monetary gain aren't reason enough for some of us to quit?

34. **Being the help** 87
If you're the one helping a mate to quit, here are some suggestions for you to take on board.

35. **Ashes to ashes** 89
It's a dirty habit. Cleaning up your act will cut down on the housework and say goodbye to airspray abuse.

36. **Join *them*** 91
The rest of the world is ganging up on smokers. Maybe it's time to throw in the towel and join the majority.

37. **Spread the word** 93
Become a single-issue bore; make non-smoking zeal your new addiction. It could be your salvation.

38. **Toothless wonder** 95
You know smoke stains your teeth. Did you know that smoking also makes your gums rot and your teeth fall out?

39. **Sex or a smoke?** 97
Would you rather give up sex or cigarettes? Sooner or later smoking is likely to win, whether you like it or not!

40. **Older and wiser** 99
With the benefit of hindsight, think about just what lessons you would be able to teach your pre-smoking self.

41. **Staying alive** 101
If you die early or become disabled through smoking you're not the only victim. Think of your family.

42. **Home sweet home** 105
Decorating your home is a great way to celebrate and reinforce your decision to quit.

43. **Smash your habit** 107
Give your ashtrays, lighters and other smoking accoutrements a death sentence. Then you've passed the point of no return.

44. **Trial separation** 109
Your relationship with cigarettes is souring. You want out. But how? Time apart might be the answer.

45. **Duty free** 111
Holiday madness. Who could possibly turn down such a bargain as half-price cigarettes? You can.

Brilliant ideas

46. **It's quiz time**.................. 113
Here's the question of a lifetime. Do you (a) keep smoking or (b) quit now or start on the road to giving up?

47. **Use hate power** 115
You've tried it all to give up but you're still puffing away. It's time to become a perverse philanthropist.

48. **Keep on quitting** 117
Quitting for good might seem like climbing Everest. Break it down into stages to make the impossible possible.

49. **Idle hands**............................ 119
With time on your hands, the addict inside you will be begging for one last cigarette. Stay active.

50. **Stay stopped**........................121
Nicotine will always be waiting to ambush you, so train yourself to become an instinctive non-smoker.

51. **One can't hurt?** 123
One cigarette isn't just one – it's the first of many. As soon as you light up you're back on the old treadmill.

52. **Dog ends** 125
Mark each day you don't smoke as it takes you further towards reclaiming your life and your health.

Introduction

If you continue to smoke throughout your adult life, there's a one in two chance that the grim reaper will take you away with a smoking-related illness or condition. Whatever pleasure you might get from smoking, those are not odds worth gambling on.

Having established what people enjoy about smoking, our book moves on to the considerable benefits of stopping. Every smoker knows the damage done by this habit, but even we were surprised to find how extensive that damage is. You know that cigarettes make your teeth yellow, but are you aware of the damage they do to your gums? You know that smoking adds a few wrinkles to your features, but did you know that a sixty-year-old smoker has the body of someone seven years older? These and other discoveries add up and are worth talking about.

Mostly, however, the book is given over to ideas to help you give up, whether it's joining a support group, using nicotine patches or other drugs, or going cold turkey. We've adopted and adapted ideas from all over the place. Some, like our suggestion for smashing up your ashtrays, are enormous fun; others, like giving money to a cause you hate if you break a pledge to stop smoking, can be pretty hairy.

There are many books around offering to help you give up, but we believe Infinite Ideas' concept is ideally suited to this subject. You will not find here a promise that if you read this book you will quit smoking. Nor are we offering a one-method-suits-all approach to giving up. Every smoker is different: what works for Fred Jones in the office may not work for Samantha Smith in the pub. Indeed, what might not have worked for Fred five years ago may now do the trick. People give up when they are ready and not a moment before. But the process can be nudged along with the suggestions, strategies and solutions you'll find here. What we offer is a huge menu to browse over and from it you can select your own quitting cocktail.

1. Hail the weed

Feel free to smoke while you read this book. We should celebrate why smoking lights us up.

Let's face it, we're addicts, aren't we? And now we can't stop. Well, in truth, we can. Fifty years ago, three out of four people smoked. Today, it's just one in four. So either a lot of people died young or lots of people quit. (Actually, it's a bit of both.) Choose which you'd rather be – dead or an ex-smoker.

We're not trying to terrify you – you know this anyway – but, just to remind ourselves what it's about before we launch into all the different ways we can give up, let's celebrate the cigarette. Smoking is relaxing. Smoking helps you concentrate. Smoking keeps you awake. It also picks you up when you're down, it calms you when you're stressed and it

Here's an idea for you

If you have a health problem visit your doctor immediately. It may not be that bad, and the doctor can put you in touch with the local smoking cessation group, who'll support you while you stop. If it is serious the earlier you catch it, the better – not knowing is more worrying than knowing the worst.

Defining idea

'It has always been my rule never to smoke when asleep, and never to refrain when awake.'
MARK TWAIN

Defining idea

'[Cigarettes are] not legitimate articles of commerce, being wholly noxious and deleterious to health. Their use is always harmful.'
TENNESSEE SUPREME COURT (upholding a total ban on cigarettes, 1898)

finishes off a job well done, a good meal, the day, lovemaking. Most smokers will say that's exactly what this wonder drug does.

And there's more to enjoying cigarettes than just the chemical hit. Cigarettes, their packets and a glittering array of fashion accessories make smoking a designer's paradise. On top of that, there's the allure of the lighters, holders and cases. Even ashtrays can be works of ceramic excellence, or reminders of some favourite distant place or football team, conjuring up the good things in our life.

Smoking is truly the complete experience. Pity it kills you at the same time. So, as you prepare to stop, relish those last few days of smoking. Really look for all the pleasures it brings you – at the same time as listing all the negatives that come with it.

2. Tobacco tribe

Persecuted smokers take comfort in numbers so giving up without alienating your smoker chums takes planning.

Smokers and non-smokers are members of different tribes. Smokers can identify abstainers as easily as if the words 'sensible non-smoker' were tattooed on their foreheads. Perhaps this is why non-smokers are never offered a cigarette. Although people do smoke in private, there is a huge social component to the habit.

One difficulty in giving up is the sense that one is letting the side down and moving in with the enemy. Instead of being a member of that cosy congregation outside the office for a smoke at the end of lunch you will be joining the smug disapprovers inside. You might be worried that once you give up you'll be barred forever from the endearing intimacy that fellow puffers share. How can you bow out and still be in the tribe?

Here's an idea for you

Stand outside your workplace with your smoking colleagues and see if you can last a tea break without lighting up. Find your own way of telling everyone you are there for their company, the gossip or the craic. If you're really struggling, you can always say you're not smoking for a bet.

> ### Defining idea
>
> *'I used to smoke two packs a day and I just hate being a non-smoker ... but I will never consider myself a non-smoker because I always find smokers the most interesting people at the table.'*
> **MICHELLE PFEIFFER**

You can learn a lot from our mate Derek, a fifty-a-day man, who was never one to go on about giving up or even cutting down. One day he stopped. 'I'm giving up for my little girl,' he said. 'It was her eighth birthday last week and I asked her what she wanted. She looked me straight in the eye and said she wanted me to quit smoking.' He was so gob-smacked that he agreed at once, and nobody could condemn that.

Having a really good reason to give up is a great way of staying in with the in crowd. You could use assertiveness techniques and just say no, but spinning a killer yarn is more fun. Beware, though, that you can still lose mates if you bang on about how wonderful everything now tastes and how much fitter you feel. Ex-smokers can reek of something far worse than stale tobacco fumes: smugness.

3. Know your foe

What kind of smoker are you? Knowing the scale of your problem helps you form a plan of action to beat the habit.

The social smoker. You only smoke at parties, Christmas, New Year and Give Up Smoking Day (because you're a free spirit and a rebel). Well, you're dicing with death – the Tobacco Demon's waiting to get you into his evil clutches. Next time you feel dangerous and want a cigarette, pause for thought before lighting up, then think again.

The casual smoker. Smokers find you baffling. So do non-smokers. You smoke once in a while (usually someone else's). Why bother? Why play Russian roulette with a deadly drug? Be good to your body and set a good example to your smoker friends. Quit now while you're ahead.

The dope smoker. Chances are that if you started smoking dope, by now you'll be hooked on a harder drug – the nicotine. We don't condone breaking the law,

Here's an idea for you

Remember those charity thermometers that showed the rising amount of cash raised? Work out roughly how much you spend on cigarettes per week. Now colour in your own thermometer week by week and see how much you've sent up in smoke.

Defining idea

'R.J. Reynolds does not – and will not – use any cigarette ingredient if scientific evaluations indicate that it will increase the inherent toxicity of tobacco smoke.'
R.J. REYNOLDS INDUSTRIES website, 2005

but if you must smoke dope take up a pipe or bong (a water pipe). Just cut out the tobacco – it's bad for your health.

The serious smoker. You smoke upwards of 20 a day. Other people's image of you is usually with a cigarette in your hand or dangling from your mouth. There's always time for just one more cigarette. You urgently need to give up. If you've never tried, believe us, it's not as hard as you might think and the benefits are enormous.

The lapsed smoker. You've lost count of the number of times you've tried to give up and failed. Don't despair; it's a tricky habit to kick. Think of your previous attempts as merely rehearsals for the big one – the time you put all your resources into the final push to kick the weed. Never give up giving up.

4. Curse Raleigh

Learn from the past and change your future. Look at the centuries of mistakes and stupidity of our smoking ancestors.

On Columbus's journey to the New World in 1492 he received 'certain dried leaves' as gifts 'much prized' by the native Arawak tribe. He threw them away. Then Rodrigo Jerez discovered tobacco smoking in Cuba and took the habit back to Spain. However, the plumes of smoke frightened his neighbours and he was imprisoned by the Holy Inquisition for seven years. But the root had taken, and on his release Jerez found that the Spanish had gone crazy for the weed. Over the next century, tobacco spread along the trade routes of the world, reaching England around 1564.

Enter the biggest Wally of them all. Taught to smoke by Sir Francis Drake, Walter Raleigh became a convert and turned on Queen Elizabeth I. He smelled money. King James I wasn't as impressed as his predecessor and in 1604 published his famous *Counterblaste to Tobacco*, describing it as a noxious weed and slapping an import tax on it. Thus big business and government for the first time

Here's an idea for you

Check out www.tobacco.org/resources/misc/losses.html to see the impressive death list Walt and his friends have contributed to over the years.

Defining idea

'Curse Sir Walter Raleigh, he was such a stupid get.'
JOHN LENNON

Defining idea

'Never let the bastard back in my room again – unless I need him.'
SAMUEL GOLDWYN

combined to make serious money out of tobacco.

Although Japan banned tobacco in 1620 and in Turkey during 1633 up to 18 people a day were executed for smoking, England, France, Spain and Italy went for the big bucks to grow and market American tobacco. Growing demand meant that the state of Virginia legalised lifelong slavery to create the manpower to work the developing tobacco plantations.

Seventeenth century doctors were already discovering some of the downsides of tobacco, linking it to several cancers. Despite this, production grew and the major tobacco companies of today were formed by the mid-nineteenth century. By 1900, 4.4 billion cigarettes were being smoked worldwide every year.

Despite growing medical evidence of the dangers of smoking, governments (taxes), big business (profits) and smokers (addiction) are so in love with tobacco that the industry has continued to grow like a cancer. The whole history, like that of most addictive drugs, is one of greed. Millions have died unnecessarily from the effects of smoking. Let's make sure we don't become just another fatal statistic.

5. The seven stages

Other smokers have given up before you. Follow the phases most of them went through.

People at stage one – *pre-contemplation* – have no intention of giving up. Why should they? As far as they're concerned, they enjoy the habit. They are denying the negative effects of smoking and can only see the advantages.

During the second phase – *contemplation* – you are increasingly aware of the risks involved in smoking but are not prepared to do anything about it. However, people who have got this far are likely to try to give up within the next six months. They are becoming increasingly aware of their addiction and may have explored alternative ways of quitting.

Preparation is the third stage. At this point the smoker wants to quit, seeing smoking as a problem that needs addressing. They may be taking active steps, like setting a quit date and thinking about support structures to help them.

Here's an idea for you

If you are content to continue smoking, we challenge you to get on the internet and have a look at the lung pictures on www.presmark.com/htmlfile/

Defining idea

'The cigarette does the smoking – you're just the sucker.'
ANON.

Good intent is replaced by an attempt to stop smoking – stage four: *action*. This phase continues until not smoking starts to feel normal, which could take anything from one to six months. During this stage you may need help coping with nicotine withdrawal and adjusting to a non-smoking lifestyle.

When you have got to level five – *maintenance* – your life starts to feel comfortable without cigarettes. You have started to master cravings and the times between these urges grow wider. Then, by stage six – *termination* – you are no longer hooked on smokes. You are conscious of what precipitates the need for a cigarette and can cope with these feelings.

Even years after stopping, 90% of ex-smokers are tempted to have a puff and may return to their old level of smoking. That's stage seven: *relapse*. Setbacks are a natural part of quitting. However far you get, once you resume smoking you are back to stage two and will have to start all over again. Knowing what stage you are at gives you a reasonable insight into your chances of giving up.

6. Imagine

Creating morbid pictures in your mind's eye can be effective in helping to put you off smoking.

We all know the dangers of smoking, but do they motivate us to stop or even cut down? Larger and larger health warnings on the side of cigarette packets could just as well be written in a foreign language for all the impact they're likely to have. On the other hand, if you are able to convert the risks into mental images, you will convert indifference into feelings and become motivated into actually doing something. See if these images resonate with you.

As you look into a packet of cigarettes try to visualise them as people – actors, musicians, people you know – who have died of lung cancer, wrapped in paper shrouds and packed into a mass grave. Then, when you light up, pause to look at the flame. Now imagine a huge flame burning up your body in a crematorium because you have died prematurely from a smoking-related illness. Imagine this every time you reach for your smokes.

Here's an idea for you

When thinking up your own smoking-related nightmare scenarios, get suggestions from friends and family. Your smoking is probably their worst nightmare.

Defining idea

'People always come up to me and say that my smoking is bothering them … well it's killing me.'

WENDY LIEBMAN, American comedian

Next time you chance across a gang of workmen resurfacing a road, check out their huge container of tar: a thick, black liquid. Imagine that stuff dripping down your throat and coating your lungs. Smokers' coughs are acquired over time. The one you have now may be no great shakes, but amplify it and imagine yourself drowning in your own fluids.

Defining idea

'So smoking is the perfect way to commit suicide without actually dying. I smoke because it's bad; it's really simple.'

DAMIEN HIRST

When you're out and about it won't be too long before you come across a lifelong smoker on their last legs, fighting for breath as though someone has placed a plastic bag over their head. See the way they smoke: relief, not pleasure; an attempt to stay calm, not cool. Imagine that's you a couple of decades hence.

7. The fat issue

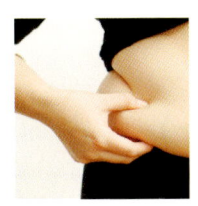

Let's think about why some, though not all, smokers gain weight after giving up and what can be done to avoid it.

Smoking dulls your taste buds, effectively smothering your meals and snacks with a blanket of nicotine. Quit smoking and your taste buds are reawakened. It's the gustatory equivalent of switching from an old black and white television to digital colour. No wonder you'll want to eat more.

Withdrawing from any substance makes you agitated. While nicotine levels in your bloodstream diminish, your body screams for a replacement chemical. And when that craving isn't met you'll start to feel jumpy. For many of us, a very effective way of shutting down this conflict between body and mind is scoffing snacks. Unwrapping a candy bar and savouring it often apes the physical movements of smoking and provides your body with a sugar

Here's an idea for you

Explore a whole range of fruits, from grapes to strawberries, melon to cherries, sultanas to bananas. Go further and check out raw carrots, celery, sunflower seeds etc. Select your favourites and use these as nibbles when you feel the need to smoke.

Defining idea

'I would rather be overweight and not smoking than underweight and dead.'
Panellist speaking to JOEL SPITZER

rush that helps it ignore the nicotine depletion. Trouble is, comfort eating only lasts as long as you chomp, and soon after your last mouthful the cravings return. Isn't life cruel?

Being able to understand what is happening helps you prepare yourself. Nervous agitation can be burnt off with aerobic exercise, like walking, swimming or cycling. In fact, exercise helps in more ways than one. Two or three bouts of serious exercise a week revs up your metabolism and releases endorphins, your body's natural uplifting, feel-good chemicals. In fact, when you exercise, your brain produces a concoction of chemicals that can help you kick the habit.

Exercise also nukes a stress substance called cortisol, chilling you out. And if that's not enough, exercise gives us warm feelings of accomplishment, cranking up self-esteem. So what? Self-esteem is instrumental in stopping smoking. Getting fit, toning up and becoming a sexy beast should help you feel a bit better about quitting. If you haven't been doing any exercise for a while, you may even find that in the process of not lighting up you actually lose weight!

8. Superkings?

Almost all smokers wish they'd never started, so how come so many of us fall into the deadly trap?

Growing up is a challenge. There are all those raging hormones, the striving for independence and the rebellion against adult authority. It's not surprising that we often head for the taboo areas, like sex, alcohol and drugs. It's a badge we can wear to say we're not kids any more.

But that's all an illusion. It's an illusion that tobacco companies, while they might say they don't take advantage of it, know all too well. They've worked wonders to create a sexy, cool image of the smoker. They create the desire in us to be just like that, like the man or the woman in the image. Trouble is, it's an advertiser's con. No question that you can be cool and sexy; what they don't mention is that you don't actually need the cigarette to achieve it.

Here's an idea for you

Talk to yourself. Improvise with a partner or write a dialogue between two versions of yourself – the Smoker and the Ex-Smoker. As an ex-addict, the latter will know all the scams, evasions and lies the Smoker will come up with to not give up just yet ... and know how to counter them.

Defining idea

'The boy who smokes cigarettes need not be anxious about his future, he has none.'
DAVID STARR JORDAN, first president of Stanford University

Smoking doesn't make you grown up, it makes you a slave and it makes you ill – maybe not today, maybe not tomorrow, but for the rest of your life. Say no, not because I say so, not because of what any adult says. Say no because you say so; because you've read some of these Ideas, gone on to the internet and done some research, because you've asked every grown-up smoker you know whether they would choose to start smoking if they were 10 or 15 or 20 again.

Take up sports, find a hobby, indulge in self-abuse – anything except start smoking. And if you're a grown-up smoker don't give up warning young smokers, whatever they say back to you. Don't just tell them not to, tell them why from your own personal experience. Cough all over them, if it helps. Even one less new smoker on the planet is better than staying silent, or offering them a cigarette.

Idea 8 – **Superkings?**

52 Brilliant Ideas - **Quit smoking for good**

9. Smoking gun

The ill effects of smoking sneak up on us. Don't ignore them or make excuses.

This is a handy guide to the smoke signals, the key things to watch out for which tell you your days may be numbered. Of course, to begin with it'll be small things, things that you feel you can cope with because they don't really seem to be doing you any major harm.

Take a good long look at yourself day by day and count the lines on your face as your habit turns you into a prematurely wrinkled prune. Your hair grows thin and loses its bounce and lustre; your fingers yellow, along with your teeth – all classic signs of a smoker.

Breathing is a brilliant idea. Your lungs really like it and so does the rest of your body. Strangling yourself is cheaper and a swifter, less painful, option than smoking. An early warning sign is the well-known smoker's cough. As time goes on, it's the breathlessness that

Here's an idea for you

Boycott the conmen. Refuse to watch or participate in any sport or cultural event sponsored by a tobacco company. Write and tell organisers and tobacco companies why you object.

Defining idea

'HIV and tobacco are the only two major causes of death that are increasing substantially throughout the world.'
RICHARD PETO, epidemiologist and statistician

hits. The stairs become a mountain and you can't run for more than a few yards. Damage your lungs and you also damage your heart, as it has to work all the harder to pump the necessary amount of oxygen to keep the muscles and vital organs going. Chest pains are a worrying sign and ought to be a serious warning that your heart just can't take it anymore.

The problems you'll be causing your blood vessels can lead to a stroke, which can kill you or leave you partially disabled or unable to speak. Classic signs are double vision, terrible headaches or difficulty finding the right words. Circulation problems can also lead to amputation, particularly of toes, feet and legs.

The only real answer is to stop now. At the very least, have regular medical check ups and go and see your doctor immediately if anything worries you. Don't give yourself a death sentence.

10. Poison cocktail

Line up for your deadly dose of poisons and see just what goes inside your body every time you light up.

How come when we buy our packet of cigarettes all we know is that we're buying tobacco, with a warning that *smoking kills*? No list of ingredients to be seen. So what is in a cigarette? Actually, it's a cocktail of over 400 toxic chemicals.

Most of us can roll out the three most obvious ingredients: **nicotine** (the substance found naturally in the tobacco plant, which is also a deadly poison and more addictive than heroin), **tar** (produced as a result of the manufacturing process of cigarettes and ingested directly into your lungs when you smoke, building up a coating on the alveoli) and **carbon monoxide** (which, in high concentrations, can kill). These are the main players, but cigarettes give you a whole lot more!

Cigarettes deliver a positive cornucopia of cancer-inducing chemicals (carcinogens), including benzene, formaldehyde, selenium,

Here's an idea for you

Write a list of what is bad about smoking. Photocopy it and pin it up in every room in the house and at work, so that you're constantly reminded.

Defining idea

'Some ingredients may be added to tobacco during manufacture for various reasons. It is our policy to assess the appropriateness and acceptability of all ingredients prior to use.'
IMPERIAL TOBACCO WEBSITE, 2005

beryllium, cadmium and nickel. These are all in use in the chemicals industry, where they are treated with the utmost caution because of the drastic effects they have on people when ingested.

Okay, so now you've set up the ideal conditions for a cancer to start growing (take your pick – lung, mouth, throat, larynx, bladder, cervix etc.). What you need now are some chemicals to help it on its way. Guess what – cigarettes provide these too.

And while we're there, let's throw in a few other toxins for good measure: ammonia, acetone, hydrogen cyanide, arsenic, lead and mercury. We bet you've heard of these and wouldn't sprinkle any on your cornflakes. So, why invite all of these chemicals into your body with every cigarette you smoke?

11. Older sooner

Seeing the impact smoking has on your face and body should give you the needed push.

As well as killing its consumers, smoking also ages them prematurely. A recent research paper found that someone smoking a packet of twenty cigarettes a day for forty years had at sixty the body of a non-smoker aged sixty-seven and a half. The evidence of the aging effect of smoking is everywhere, even staring out of the chap you shave in the morning or the woman to whose face you apply lipstick.

The question then becomes how you can convert insights like these into motivation providing the impetus to help you quit. So, why not get an advanced view of what you'll become sooner rather than later if you keep smoking?

Here's an idea for you

Talk to a selection of children and teenagers who don't know anything about you (if you dare). Ask them to tell you how old you are – the first number that occurs to them, not a figure to flatter you. You may be shocked to discover that this group think you're older than you are. Adults are more likely to tell you what they think you want to hear.

Defining idea

'One only dies once, and it's for such a long time.'
MOLIÈRE

You can get a painful image of your future using a computer software tool like Photoshop to manipulate a picture of yourself. There are sure to be plenty of people who'd be willing to take this project on for you. With a little imagination they can yellow your teeth, make your skin more flawed and accentuate the other tell-tale signs of aging.

In many shopping malls and tourist traps you can find an artist sitting behind an easel waiting to draw your portrait. They usually draw flattering likenesses of their sitters but your purpose is to commission a portrait that adds a decade or two to how you look now. Say that you want to see what you will look like in ten or twenty years' time.

Defining idea

'My face looks like a wedding cake left out in the rain.'
W.H. AUDEN

Annotate your portentous picture with the words: *stopping smoking will slow down the time it takes me to get to this*. Then frame it and hang it in a prominent place at home.

12. Tobacco giants

Someone out there is getting very rich – at your expense – selling a deadly drug. Let's find out who.

This story is set in Tobaccoland, which is ruled over by six greedy giants. They are called British American Tobacco, Philip Morris Incorporated, R.J. Reynolds Industries, The Rembrandt Group, American Brands Inc. and Imperial Tobacco Limited. Between them they rule the world. Today they have 1.3 billion slaves who all smoke their evil weed. They don't mention the 70 million people who died in the last half century from smoking, or the 100 million expected to die over the next 30 years.

As the slaves grew older they died early from horrible diseases. So the giants began looking to enslave the young – with any luck, these might live 30 or 40 years before they die. They also searched for new slaves in countries far beyond their borders. They never think how much extra in health costs they're burdening these poor countries with.

Here's an idea for you

Jot down your ideas for an advert for cigarettes knowing that you want people to give you as much money as possible to help them kill themselves more quickly. Send a copy to every tobacco company you can find for comment.

Defining idea

'One of the prime activities of [the tobacco] industry is in effect to act as a tax collector for the government, who will proceed very cautiously before they kill the goose which lays such a big golden egg.'
SIR DAVID NICHOLSON, Euro MP and former chairman of Rothmans International

Defining idea

'Tobacco addiction is a disease communicated through advertising, sports, marketing and sponsorship. This is not a free choice at all.'
GRO HARLEM BRUNDTLAND, World Health Organization

It took about 300 years for the slaves to realise that the evil weed was in fact poisoning them. They wanted to overthrow the giants. However, the giants found some good friends – governments. The governments were as greedy as the giants. They saw how rich the giants had become from the evil weed and decided that they, too, wanted a share, so they made the giants give them half of everything they made from the weed. When the people asked their government for help, the government said no.

13. Spot the pitch

Knowing how tobacco is marketed might not help you give up, but at least you'll know what you're up against.

You have to admire these guys, who are clearly top of their class: selling tobacco is some challenge. It's a product nobody really needs – who really wants to spend tons of money to get yellow teeth, brown fingers, wrinkled skin and messed up fitness? So, how did they do it?

For a start, they aimed to get 'em young. While it would be difficult to prove that cigarette barons and their advertisers actually target kids, they do go after the impressionable, which, with no disrespect to the young, is more or less the same thing. After all, how many people can you name who took up smoking in their thirties or beyond?

Here's an idea for you

Start your own counter-advertising campaign. Next time you see a cigarette advert, try to mentally replace it with your counter-image. Cut out photos of stars who have died of smoking-related illnesses and superimpose yellow teeth and brown fingers.

Defining idea

'Every Marlboro ad needs to be judged on the following criteria: story value, authenticity, masculinity, while communicating those enduring core values of freedom, limitless opportunities, self-sufficiency, mastery of destiny and harmony with nature.'
PHILIP MORRIS INCORPORATED

In the early decades of the twentieth century, cigarette manufacturers were quick to sign up sports stars and big screen idols. Even before young men were old enough to buy cigarettes for themselves they would pester parents for cigarette cards with pictures of footballers, cricketers or boxers. Forging links between cigarettes and success was a masterstroke. Reinforce this with Hollywood glamour and suddenly smoking becomes sexy as well as cool.

While we all like to believe that we're unaffected by adverts, it's always worth challenging this type of propaganda. Look at a few common messages and misconceptions and add some counter-spin.

Smoking is sensual, they say. Actually, smelling of smoke is a turn-off. *Non-smokers are losers*. Nope, they're richer, healthier and less wrinkly. *Smokers have more fun*. Sure, if your idea of fun is having more strokes and looking on average a decade older than non-smokers. *Smoking makes you more attractive*. To advertisers and cigarette barons, maybe.

14. How much?!

You pay through the nose for your habit. Look at the hidden costs of smoking and you're even worse off.

I have smoked for a total of … years, and I spend … each week on tobacco. By totting this up you discover the staggering sum that you have handed over to the shops and, indirectly, tobacco barons and the taxman since you were a teenager. Perhaps you've already done this exercise, been shocked, but rationalised it as almost a third of the adult population is in the same boat.

We know you're not stupid and already know how much smoking costs you each week. However, there's no easy way to say this, but the harsh truth is even worse. There are many more indirect ways smoking hits your pocket. Life insurance companies, for instance, offer smokers a higher premium or give non-smokers a discount. It boils down to the same thing: puffers pay more.

Here's an idea for you

Sit down with a pen and paper and someone who really knows you and work out the real cost of smoking. Be as honest as you can, taking account of as many hidden costs as possible. Having arrived at a monthly or yearly total, visualise what you would use this sum for: foreign travel, replacing the old banger or more booze.

Defining idea

'Our objective is to maximize prices, such that we exceed cost base increases, while avoiding undesired margin scrutiny by the authorities whenever threatened.'
PHILIP MORRIS INCORPORATED, Internal memo

Then there are extra dry-cleaning bills. If you smoke, your clothes will need to be washed or dry cleaned more frequently than if you don't. And if you want to see the effect smoking has on the paintwork, just walk into any pub. Non-smoking households stay pristine longer. Also, there are the costs of cover ups: peppermints, air fresheners etc.

In reality, these concrete examples only take you to the foothills of what your addiction actually costs. If time is money, how much have you lost in cigarette breaks? Give your boss the impression that you are always popping out for a cigarette break and you might just get passed over for a vital promotion. And if the habit results in reduced health and fitness, what price then?

15. Time to quit

Waiting until you feel completely committed to giving up is as futile as herding cats.

Almost everyone wants to give up smoking sometimes: usually, a time other than now. It could be for any number of reasons: cost, health grounds, effect on physical appearance, to silence a disapproving partner, stigma or a cocktail of any of these. If this is true, it should follow that more people ought to be giving up than actually are. Sadly, we are programmed not only to avoid pain or discomfort, but also to defer it as long as possible.

Ambivalence about stopping means that most of us put all the good reasons for wanting to give up on the back burner and use its flame to light up what we kid ourselves will be one of our last cigarettes. The time to stop, we tell ourselves, is not quite now: tomorrow I will feel stronger about quitting; I will have more motivation and will be less likely to buckle under.

Here's an idea for you

Start a diary of setbacks and other disappointments so that you can whip up enough bad temper and passion to quit. We reckon you won't have to wait long before the feel-bad factor grows sufficiently for you to kick the habit.

Defining idea

'Thank heaven I have given up smoking again! ... God I feel fit. Homicidal but fit. A different man. Irritable, moody, depressed, rude, nervy, perhaps; but the lungs are fine.'
A. P. HERBERT

Defining idea

'Cigarettes are killers that travel in packs.'
ANON.

This brings us to a profoundly important idea: *the best time to quit smoking is when you're feeling shit*. This simple statement might sound counter-intuitive – arse about face to the rest of us – but think back to those times when anger gave you the energy and concentration to carry out a job you would otherwise avoid: sorting out the junk in the garage when the shelves gave way or organising your files after you failed to find that letter from your accountant.

One of the great things about using disappointments, disasters and setbacks, major or minor, to fuel your ambition to give up is that they generally come along at regular intervals. On the other hand, if you just wait for success to arrive you might be waiting forever. Honestly, *the best time to quit smoking is when you're feeling shit*.

16. Diversion ahead

Willpower alone may not be enough. Discovering ploys to distract yourself from cravings can prevent a relapse.

You've taken the plunge, decided to stop again. Somehow you've managed to get through the first day. You're feeling pretty pleased with yourself but sooner rather than later the cravings come: 'just one little ciggie can't hurt,' the sirens call. You're tempted.

Can cravings be stopped? *No.* But you can learn to cope with them and continue to quit using strategies that have worked for others. The cravings might be triggered by a setback or frustration. However, they might also surface when you find yourself doing something where you'd usually be lighting up – after a meal, perhaps, or being in the company of smokers.

Here's an idea for you

Draw a table with three columns: one for *when* you smoke; the second for *why* you're smoking then; and the third for your *alternative* (non-smoking) ways of getting the same result. Your partner or someone who knows you well could help. When thinking of the non-smoking alternatives, try to be as creative as possible, but make sure that they are achievable, sustainable and, most importantly, not punitive.

Defining idea

'I phoned my dad to tell him I had stopped smoking. He called me a quitter.'
STEVEN PEARL

You need to be prepared for these craving-precipitators and plan how you are going to react to them. You can do this in three stages. First, list the times and places that usually trigger you to light up. Next, for each time or place, describe the reasons why you smoke. Then think of a non-smoking alternative.

For instance, that first cigarette of the day is one you're gasping for but there may be other reasons why you crave it. Perhaps you stand outside the house and use the time to contemplate the day ahead. Perhaps you also enjoy escaping the mayhem of the rest of the family scrambling to get ready for school or work. So, what's an alternative? You could go for a walk and still use this time to think through problems alone and mentally prepare yourself for the day. Experiment with gum or fruit to see if it helps.

17. Suck it and see

Help is at hand. Nicotine replacement therapy (NRT) is available at the chemist's or on prescription.

Cigarettes are simply the means of feeding your nicotine addiction. The good news is that a variety of alternative methods have been devised to give you your nicotine hit in ways that can break the link with cigarettes and can wean you off the weed. These products are not cheap and can work out as expensive as smoking, even on prescription, but given that you will only need to use them for about three months, it is worth thinking of them as a wise investment.

Nicotine chewing gum is great because it gives you a nicotine fix where and when you need it. Your body takes in nicotine through your gums as you chew. It's best to think of the gum as a medication to be taken regularly every hour or so. Nicotine patches give you a

Here's an idea for you

Wherever you live there is likely to be a smoking cessation service not too far away that offers either individual or group therapy. In the UK these services are often run by the NHS. Check one out and see what advice and support it offers for people wishing to try NRT.

Defining idea

'A cigarette is the perfect type of a perfect pleasure. It is exquisite and it leaves one unsatisfied. What more can one want?'
OSCAR WILDE, The Picture of Dorian Gray

constant flow of nicotine through your skin. It's a good idea to move them to a different patch of skin every day so that they don't provoke a skin reaction.

If gum and patches aren't your style, microtabs could be just the thing. All you need to do is hold one under your tongue until it fizzles away to nothing. If you suck, chew or swallow, you'll diminish the dose and they won't work. If you really can't resist sucking your microtabs, ditch them in favour of nicotine lozenges. Just don't chew.

Defining idea

'Nicotine patches are great. Stick one over each eye and you can't find your cigarettes.'
ANON.

Some hardcore smokers need something more – a nicotine nasal spray. It's the strongest form of nicotine replacement out there and, as the nicotine is absorbed through the lining of your nose, it works very quickly.

18. Cold turkey

A short, sharp shock or a phased withdrawal? A case can be made either way.

Think back to your days at school and swimming lessons in the outdoor, unheated pool. Given that you haven't got a hope in hell of getting out of the lesson, do you (a) put off full immersion as long as possible, dipping your goose-pimpled body gradually deeper into the cold, or (b) dive in and get the traumatic business over with in one unpleasant hit? That knowledge might indicate whether you're temperamentally better suited to cold turkey or gradual cessation of smoking.

With cold turkey, it's a clean break. You and other people know where you are: you can be regarded as a non-smoker and send out clear messages that you don't want to be offered a smoke or given any encouragement to resume. You can also throw out ashtrays, lighters and everything to do with your old habit. Having to replace these things might just boost your waning resolve.

Here's an idea for you

You've gone cold turkey and are over the worst. Great. Why not celebrate by throwing a post-smoking party? It is reckoned to take thirty days to create a new habit, so book a date a month after you've given up and use the occasion to thank your support team for getting you through the worst.

Defining idea

'I know a man who gave up smoking, drinking, sex, and rich food. He was healthy right up to the day he killed himself.'
JOHNNY CARSON

Another plus for cold turkey is that you will get all your unpleasant symptoms over in one hit and you can make harm limitation contingencies to help you over the hump. This way your body knows what's happening. Bodies find it hard to cope with being in a state of limbo: you either smoke or you don't.

Faced with withdrawal symptoms, people who attempt to cut down often self-medicate by lighting up again. Not a problem for cold turkeys. However, suddenly stopping can make some people impossible to live with. It's a shock to the system that is just too much for them. This might be more psychological than physical, but it's still too much to cope with and a gradual cessation might work better.

Idea 18 – **Cold turkey**

52 Brilliant Ideas – **Quit smoking for good**

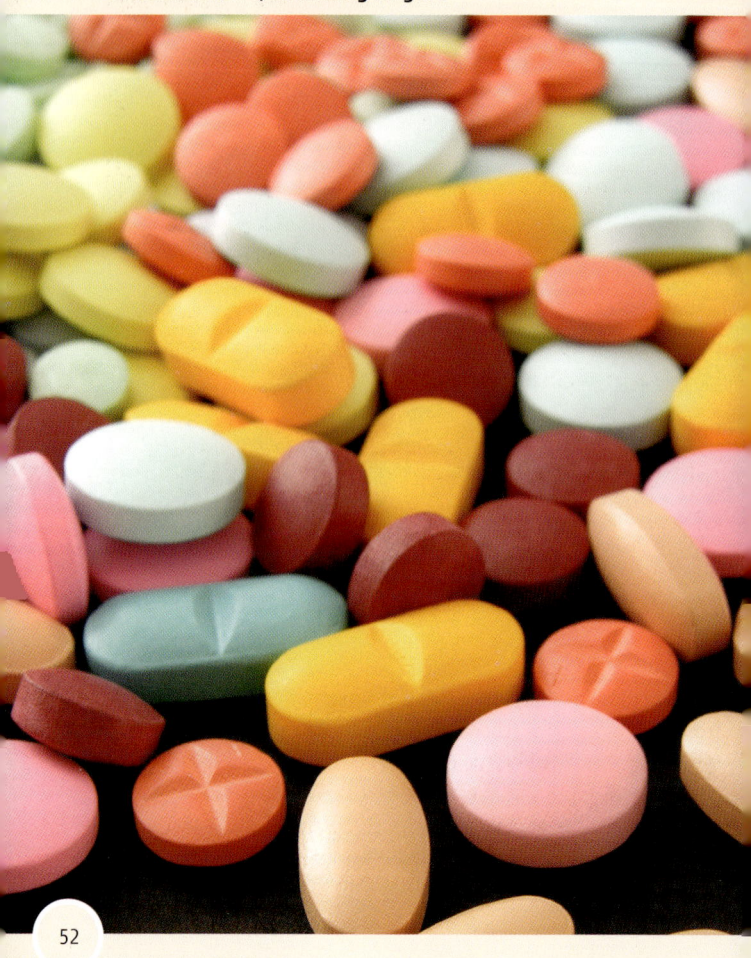

19. Super drugs

Discover a drug that effectively curbs cravings and reduces withdrawals.

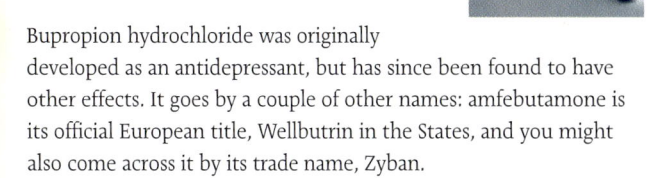

Bupropion hydrochloride was originally developed as an antidepressant, but has since been found to have other effects. It goes by a couple of other names: amfebutamone is its official European title, Wellbutrin in the States, and you might also come across it by its trade name, Zyban.

Although bupropion was being used as an antidepressant when doctors discovered it reduced nicotine withdrawal symptoms, you definitely don't have to be depressed to use it, and if it works you won't be depressed afterwards either. It's important that we're up-front and make it clear that it won't eliminate all your withdrawal symptoms – but it will make them weaker; so much so that many people are blissfully unaware of them. It's totally different from nicotine replacement therapy because it doesn't contain any nicotine. And, unlike NRT, you can only get it on prescription.

Here's an idea for you

You've set your quit date. That's brilliant. Now make another date, this time with your doctor, to talk through the pros and cons of bupropion and work out the best time to start taking it.

Defining idea

'I went on Zyban about two years ago and it worked for me. I didn't have any side effects at all. It just made you forget to smoke. I have the occasional cigarette now but I'll never go back to fifteen a day.'

MARTIN CHEUNG, computer engineer and former smoker

Sadly, this isn't the sort of tablet you can take once and forget about while it does its stuff. Here's how it goes. You'll start taking one 150 mg tablet of bupropion a week before your stop date to make sure a decent amount of drug is active in your bloodstream by the time you quit. A day or so prior to your stopping date, your doctor will probably advise you to increase your daily dose to two tablets. You'll continue to take two tablets for the next seven to eleven weeks, depending on your doctor's advice.

There are pros and cons to taking any drug. In the UK, out of 513,000 people who have been on bupropion, 58 have died taking it. This is why it's important to work closely with your doctor to weigh up the bupropion balance.

20. Smoke screen

Beating nicotine reliance is the easy bit. Defeating the psychological web of addiction beneath is a tougher task.

The Tobacco Demon is a powerful enemy and he feeds off you. But he's inside your head – a creation of your own making. He comes as part of every smoking addict's kit. He, far more than the poison nicotine, keeps you being a smoker or waylays you years after you've quit.

He comes across as a sympathetic friend who understands you, the smoker. He readily agrees that it's hard to give up smoking (so why bother?). He's aware that smoking is bad for you (so why not just cut down a bit?). He knows it's difficult to stay stopped (so why not just have one?). He wants you to stay an addict. He'll support all your reasons for how stopping smoking will make life more difficult – you'll get irritable, you'll become fat, all your friends still smoke …

You need to know your enemy within and sever the hold he has over you. The Tobacco Demon feeds

Here's an idea for you

Write a letter to every tobacco company. Tell them you are addicted to cigarettes and you think that it may be bad for your health. Ask their advice on how to stop.

Defining idea

'Tobacco that outlandish weede
It spends the braine and spoiles the seede
It dulls the spirite, it dims the sight
It robs a woman of her right.'
WILLIAM VAUGHAN, poet and colonial pioneer

off all the mini-habits and rituals that make up your smoking. They are your weaknesses, and he haunts them day and night. Round up your usual suspects, the ones that act as triggers for you to smoke, and then you'll know when to fight the Demon. Chant your mantra: 'I don't smoke, I don't smoke. I'm not a slave and I want to live.'

The Tobacco Demon can deliver his deadly weapons within seconds, just as long as it takes to get you to reach for the pack and light up. Whenever you get that urge, stop. Stop for ten seconds. Think what you're doing. If you've picked up any of the brilliant ideas here, go for it and use your defences – nicotine gum, meditation, whatever it is. Pause for thought and save your life.

21. Air equals life

Simple fact: without air we die. So, how can anyone in their right mind choose to screw up their airways?

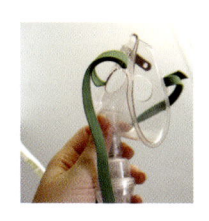

When we smoke, tar enters our airways through our mouth and throat, then travels down into the lungs. This tar that we send down with every lungful of smoke steadily coats everything in a black sticky slime. Oxygen has great difficulty breaking through it, with the result that smokers get 15% less oxygen than everyone else. And the heart has to crank up its action to keep everything working. Eventually the build-up of tar will become so great that breathing becomes really difficult and as a result we become less and less mobile.

There's no such thing as a safe cigarette, so it's no use deluding ourselves that one cigarette is less hazardous than another. When filters were introduced, the idea was broadcast that not only did they improve the flavour, but they also filtered out many of the

Here's an idea for you

Take a slightly damp tissue. Light a cigarette and then breathe all your smoke out directly through the tissue until you've finished. This is what goes into your lungs every time you light up.

Defining idea

'In Britain about 90% of all lung cancer and emphysema is caused by smoking, and about 20% of coronary heart disease.'
MARTIN RAW, Kick the Habit

harmful effects. They don't. Although there may be a difference in taste between a 'full flavour' cigarette and a 'light' and a difference in the tar yield, it makes no real difference to their comparative safety. No cigarette is safe – they'll all kill you.

There's no such thing as safer smoking. The only safe way to smoke is not to. You can make a very tiny difference by not smoking the cigarette down to the end or taking fewer puffs, but that's really a con. You'll probably just end up smoking two or three extra cigarettes to make up for it, so you're no better off.

Don't fool yourself. There is no get-out clause. Smoking kills and that's that. Damage your lungs and you'll destroy your body.

22. The alternatives

'New age' treatments are worth a try. Most have been around far longer than cigarettes and draw on ancient wisdom.

Ever thought you'd be sticking needles in yourself to stop being a drug addict? Well, acupuncture has the painless answer: tackle the addiction, relieve stress and improve your sleep patterns. Those needles have a point. They operate on a pattern of energy lines running through the body that have key points, like junctions in a power system. In treating smoking, the professional acupuncturist can change the energy flow to provide valuable assistance in reducing both your craving and the tensions that come with giving up.

Sneak up on your habit and tackle it while it's not looking – with hypnosis. Talking to your subconscious could help root out the underlying causes of your addiction and give you hidden support. Once you are in a hypnotised state, your mind is open to suggestion, and a skilled hypnotist will plant subtle counter-triggers in your mind to ward off

Here's an idea for you

Join a gym or take up a regular exercise routine. Working your body triggers the release of endorphins into your bloodstream, which creates a natural high.

Defining idea

'More doctors smoke Camels than any other cigarette!'
R.J. REYNOLDS INDUSTRIES advertising slogan, 1946

your desire for cigarettes. It can also help to generally relax you and bring down your stress levels.

Yoga in itself is not a direct method for giving up smoking, but it can prove to be a very useful ally. What it can offer is a method of increasing the flow of endorphins through the body, creating a deep sense of well-being, which is both relaxing and energising. It's rather like creating a still pool in your life, and once you have learned a few positions it can be practised any time. Many leisure centres have yoga classes. Similar claims could be made for meditation, which focuses on breathing. It's a great alternative to a smoke and gives you a natural high. Both yoga and meditation are relatively low-cost options.

Defining idea

'More than 34 million working days are lost each year because of smoking-related sick leave.'
www.patient.co.uk

It's worth sampling a range of these alternative therapies to see what mix works for you so check out your nearest complementary medicine centre, or ask your doctor for what's available in your neighbourhood.

23. First of the day

You want it simple? This is it: never smoke your first cigarette of the day again and you've stopped for ever.

There is a theory that smoking cigarettes is not a habit, it's a series of habits. We don't simply smoke cigarettes arbitrarily. Each one has a trigger, a link to some action or routine. Look at the different kinds of cigarettes we smoke during the day.

For most of us, the first cigarette of the day is our favourite. Nicotine levels are low after a night's sleep so the hit is all the sweeter. Many of us will smoke a cigarette almost before we do anything else with our day. This is a tricky one to give up. Another toughie is the one (or more) we smoke on the way to work to prepare ourselves for the tasks ahead (plus we know we may not get a cigarette break for another hour or two).

The external discipline of a workplace is great for us as smokers: we're not allowed to smoke. The

Here's an idea for you

Keep a log of all the cigarettes you smoke in a week. Note what time you light up and what event/opportunity it's connected to. Recognising the problem times is the first step to curing them.

Defining idea

'I like you more than I would like to have a cigarette.'
WENDY COPE, Giving Up Smoking

moment we can, we do – not necessarily because we want to but simply because it's permitted at break time. And, of course, there's the cup of coffee – it has to be accompanied by a cigarette or it's just not the same.

Another danger time is after eating. Our defences are down and next thing we know we have a lit cigarette in our hand. It's the same if we're enjoying a leisurely drink with friends. Our ingrained pattern of behaviour automatically clicks in and triggers one 'pleasure' to go with another. And then the day is done; time to wind down before bed. What better relaxant than a goodnight cigarette?

There will be lots of other specific habitual cigarettes you'll be able to identify as you begin to analyse your personal smoker's profile. Tackle them one by one – corner the enemy then go for the jugular.

24. Climb the ladder

Some people stop but start again over years. Even when they don't smoke, at heart they still feel like smokers.

Imagine a day in the future when you are an ex-smoker. How will you know that things are going well? What will you be doing differently that will indicate that something has happened this time that hasn't happened before? If you are not smoking, what will you be spending your time on instead? If you're not having to cough up for the cigarettes, how will you use the extra money?

Now imagine a ladder with ten rungs. The top rung represents your life as an ex-smoker and the bottom or first rung is the opposite – chain smoking all day and getting up several times at night to smoke. Where do you place yourself on this ladder? It is likely that you are somewhere in between, neither rock bottom nor at the top. The mere fact

Here's an idea for you

To make the climb more vivid, design your own bespoke smokes and ladders board, with a zig-zag path from the bottom of the board to the top. In ascending order, grade all the stages between being a confirmed smoker and ex-smoker on the top. Include a few snakes (or smokes) for occasional relapses.

Defining idea

'To cease smoking is the easiest thing I ever did. I ought to know because I've done it a thousand times.'
MARK TWAIN (attributed)

Defining idea

'I'm not really a heavy smoker any more. I only get through two lighters a day now.'
BILL HICKS, American comedian

that you haven't got a foot on the floor is grounds for hope: it suggests that there are times that you are coping without smoking.

Take a few minutes to jot down what has helped you rise from the bottom rung to your present one and what stops you descending, especially in times of stress. This is the secret of your success and using it consciously could be the key to cracking the smoking habit. Now ask yourself what will tell you when you have moved up a rung or two. And finally, ask yourself how you will know when you have reached the top of the ladder.

When you've worked your way through this, you'll have a list of your strengths, skills and abilities as an ex-smoker. If you keep repeating the exercise at intervals, you'll be enjoying the view from the top before you even know it.

Idea 24 – **Climb the ladder**

52 Brilliant Ideas – **Quit smoking for good**

25. Words on paper

Keeping a record of your struggle to quit will help you stay on track and give you something to be proud of.

If you already record your private thoughts and feelings in a diary you won't need us to convince you about the many virtues of this sort of record keeping, nor the therapy and release it provides. Giving up smoking is a life-changing event, and the account of your campaign deserves to be recorded, even if you will be the only person who sees it.

Putting pen to paper or fingers to a keyboard provides an opportunity to reflect and process what is happening to you. Sometimes in the course of writing down a difficulty, a solution will emerge from somewhere inside. For example, by recording your fear that you will surrender to the urge to 'just have one', that anxiety might be replaced by resolve to carry on.

Here's an idea for you

Even if you are still smoking, start a diary today. Record your hopes and fears, anticipated difficulties and anything else related to smoking or giving up. Invest in a ring binder and paper or create a folder on your computer, whatever suits you best.

Defining idea

'I always say, keep a diary and some day it'll keep you.'
MAE WEST

Defining idea

'I never travel without my diary. One should always have something sensational to read on the train.'
OSCAR WILDE, The Importance of Being Earnest

Used effectively, diaries are supporters and collaborators in the struggle against smoking. Keep one for a couple of weeks and you'll start to notice patterns. Some times of the week you'll manage to go without smoking for hours or even days. Once you've pinpointed them, doing more of whatever it is you do at those times is a great way of staying stopped for longer.

Of course, keeping a tally of smoked cigarettes can be frightening when you realise just how many you have got through, but this doesn't have to be a bad thing. At least you'll know what you're up against and what you need to work on.

Over the months, your diary will be a great gauge of how your quitting is progressing, and you'll be able to use it to track your recovery and predict what you need to do to get through those times of temptation. And, should the worst happen and you relapse, these notes will provide vital evidence that you can learn from.

26. Beat the weed

Familiar behaviour is full of triggers for the smoking reflex. Change the patterns and flummox the Tobacco Demon.

Note the order in which you do things in the morning. Change it. So, if your normal routine is shower, dress, coffee and cigarette, then off to work, change it to orange juice with the newspaper, then shower and dress. Changing the routine means you disrupt the ritual triggers. If you smoke twenty a day but only start at midday you stand a better chance of stopping than someone who only smokes ten a day but lights up first thing.

If you drive to work, make a rule: no smoking in the car. If you live close to work, cycle or walk, and remember to forget your cigarettes. If you take the bus or the train, take a newspaper or good novel and bury yourself in that. Make a rule: no smoking on the platform or in the bus queue.

Here's an idea for you

If you can't give up all at once (cold turkey), try delaying that first cigarette of the day. Build up in blocks of 10 or 15 minutes each day.

Defining idea

'Now the only thing I miss about sex is the cigarette afterward. It tasted so good that even if I had been frigid I would have pretended otherwise just to be able to smoke it.'
FLORENCE KING

Don't go outside with the smokers during work breaks. Change your drink if tea or coffee triggers the cigarette habit. Read your book, listen to music, find something practical to do with your hands. At home, make the dining room a non-smoking zone. Enjoy a new drink after the meal as your pleasurable reward for avoiding the post-prandial puff. When you're out and about in restaurants or bars, go with non-smokers if you can. If you can't, don't be tempted into accepting a cigarette, and resist any temptation to go and stand outside in the rain!

Defining idea

'Coffee and tobacco are complete repose.'
TURKISH PROVERB

Avoid the last smoke of the day by distracting yourself. Have a list of daily must-do jobs around the home or take up a new hobby (particularly one that uses the hands). Set yourself an amount of time for these activities and the chances are you'll have passed the critical moment of the urge to smoke by bedtime.

27. Feel lucky?

We know smoking's a risky business, but just how does it compare with other life-threatening activities?

There are lies, damned lies and statistics. That said, we all use them in assessing life's risks. Take a group of 1,000 average 20-year-old smokers and see what life holds in store for them. Of these 250 will die from smoking-related diseases between 35 and 69 and 250 will die from smoking-related diseases in old age. In effect, if you smoke, you have a one in two chance of dying from it.

Have no fear of flying. Your chance of coming down in flames without a parachute is only 1 in 10,000,000. That's an awful lot of holidays in the sun before your number's up. The open road gets a bit scarier. Car accidents lurch down to a somewhat unnerving 1 in 600. And, whatever you do, don't get on a motorbike – on one of those, your chances slump to 1 in 50.

Here's an idea for you

Explore the internet and give yourself a scare. Type into your search engine words like 'tobacco-related diseases', 'emphysema', 'lung cancer'. Download and read at your leisure.

Defining idea

'It's now proved beyond doubt that smoking is one of the leading causes of statistics.'
FLETCHER KNABEL, American journalist and writer

Then we come to cigarette smokers, predictably high on the list. If you smoke a pack a day, insurers give you a 1 in 25 chance of dying in the next ten years. And this increases the longer you've smoked and the older you get.

People die every day – most from disease or accident, but some of us apparently through choice. Suicide by smoking is top of the class. Every year in the UK there are 2,000 deaths from infectious diseases, 3,000 from cirrhosis of the liver, 4,000 from actual suicide and 4,000 from road accidents. Top of the heap though are the smokers. Around 120,000 of us go up in smoke each year.

So weigh up the odds. If you stop smoking before 35 your life expectancy is only slightly less than people who've never smoked. If you stop before 50 your risk drops by half. And it's never too late to stop. If you do, you'll definitely live longer – racing certainty.

28. Indiscriminate

Prince or pauper, millionaire or milkman – tobacco ruthlessly slays any of its users.

Smoking is such a widespread habit that it's easy to ignore just how lethal long-term use can be. One way of bringing home this message is considering the effect cigarettes have had on people you have heard of – people in the public eye.

There are websites that list the names of famous people who have died of a smoking-related condition. One long list is full of personalities from all parts of show business and public life: Louis Armstrong from the world of jazz; Lucille Ball and Jack Benny some will remember from childhood telly; Gary Cooper, Clark Gable and Steve McQueen from Hollywood; Ian Fleming, F. Scott Fitzgerald and Dashiell Hammett batting for the writers; Princess Margaret representing the royals and so on and on.

What makes lists like this extra depressing is that everyone on them was mega-rich; they were able to afford the best medical advice,

Here's an idea for you

Overexposure to government health warnings can make you immune to them. Compensate for this by making up your own health warnings based on smoking-related illnesses that run in your family or those your icons have succumbed to.

Defining idea

'On CBS Radio the news of Ed Murrow's death, reportedly from lung cancer, was followed by a cigarette commercial.'
ALEXANDER KENDRICK

treatment and care, yet nothing they could buy made a jot of difference in the end. Good terminal medical and nursing care is no replacement for a healthy old age.

Rather than just leaving this as a simple list, find out more about each subject to look for parallels with your own habit. What specifically did they die of? How old were they? And were they moderate or serious smokers?

Defining idea

'I don't want to achieve immortality through my work ... I want to achieve it through not dying.'
WOODY ALLEN

Knowing the plight of so many rich and famous smokers is of itself unlikely to stop you smoking. However, the gradual build up of this knowledge can add to your resolve, especially when it's allied to other strategies.

29. Smell of success

When quitting seems impossible, it's time to remind yourself that there are myriad smokers who *have* stopped.

You can get so depressed about the information you find in newspapers, books and magazines about the havoc that smoking is doing to your health, your relationships and your pocket that you might be tempted to give up reading. Before you do, spare a few minutes while we trawl through our successful quitters file and revisit a case history of someone we know who has put the smoking habit behind him.

Arvid started smoking back in the early seventies while a 19-year-old bandsman in the British Army. Cheap cigarettes were one of the few perks of the job. In the three decades since, Arvid estimates that he tried to give up at least twenty times. His latest decision to stop was because he was tired of the coughing, the breathlessness and other deleterious impacts on his health.

Here's an idea for you

Ex-smokers are everywhere – people who were once as hooked as you are now. Talk to non-smoking friends and colleagues and you'll discover that many of them were once moderate or even heavy smokers. Ask them how and why they stopped, whether they still get the odd craving and what they do about it, and what advice they would give to someone contemplating giving up. Learn from their experience.

Defining idea

'I didn't give up cigarettes, I was so ill I couldn't smoke. I just never started again.'
KEITH WATERHOUSE, journalist and novelist

He recently finished his second course of the smoking cessation drug Zyban. He first tried it six years ago, but got frightened off by an article in a newspaper that suggested people taking this medication were dropping like flies. But this time he wasn't put off by Zyban scare stories. The drug worked, and after twelve weeks he was down to a single tablet every five days. Since finishing the course he hasn't restarted smoking.

During past attempts, giving up made him bad tempered and irritable, and even staunch non-smoker friends and family would plead with him to restart. But this wasn't the case this time. Arvid has also been gratified by the positive support he has received from other ex-smokers – many of them virtual strangers.

30. Phone a friend

Finding the right person to help you quit could be the difference between success and failure.

The problems faced by smokers trying to give up are akin to those encountered by someone running for public office. A solution for politicians – getting a campaign manager – is one that can be adapted to your own campaign. If you live in the UK you could refer yourself to your nearest NHS quit-line service. There are also private counsellors offering one-to-one help, but they usually come at a price and we reckon that it shouldn't be too difficult to find and nurture your own cessation coach.

The qualities needed to help someone give up smoking are many and varied. If you can find someone who really wants to help you quit, is patient, calm under pressure, can see the wood from the trees and can help you discover creative solutions, then you're on to a winner.

Here's an idea for you

Before you phone a friend and ask for help in quitting, sit down and write a 'job spec' for them. This will need to include what you expect from your friend as a coach, how they can help, whether you'll have prearranged meetings or you just need someone who'll respond to crises.

Defining idea

'The cigarette is a portable therapist.'
TERRI GUILLEMENTS

Why would they want to help you? We suggest that you show them a list of compelling reasons why quitting will improve life for you and those around you. Persuade them that giving up is going to be really tough for you and that their help will be vital to keep you on track. Specify their unique qualities and what you hope their role could be.

Defining idea

'I'm glad I don't have to explain to a man from Mars why each day I set fire to dozens of little pieces of paper, and put them in my mouth.'
MIGNON MCLAUGHLIN

Does your coach need to be an ex-smoker? Having someone who has successfully completed the process certainly helps, as they'll have first-hand experience of what you are going through and are living evidence that it can be done. On the other hand, different qualities possessed by a lifelong non-smoker could outweigh their lack of experience. After all, you don't expect your doctor to have suffered with every bug before you go and consult her.

31. Shared air

There are almost always people around you when you smoke. What are you doing to them?

There's been a lot of debate about whether inhaling someone else's smoke can be harmful, even if you're not a smoker yourself. Recent research has shown, however, that it's extremely dangerous. You are 20–30% more likely to suffer from heart disease and diseases of the blood vessels if you regularly breathe in other people's cigarette smoke. Those at most risk are the partners or children of smokers, particularly if you regularly smoke in the same room or car as them. They haven't decided to smoke, you've chosen for them.

To see the danger, you only have to look at the number of people who have died from smoking-related diseases simply because they work in a smoky workplace, like a pub or club. They're subjected to an atmosphere that is thick with the poisons from smoking and have no option but to breathe it in. Don't force it on them.

Here's an idea for you

Limit yourself to only smoking when you're absolutely alone and outside. Make a rule never to smoke in an enclosed space again. Buy a warm raincoat if it's winter, because you'll have to battle the elements as well as your addiction.

Defining idea

'An estimated 17,000 children in the UK under 5 are hospitalised each year for chest infections related to parents' smoking.'
GASP SMOKE FREE SOLUTIONS, 'Passive Smoking: The Facts' leaflet

Two out of three people now say that being in a smoky room bothers them. Smoke affects the eyes, nose and throat. It can lead to coughs, nausea, dizziness or headaches in non-smokers plus it makes asthma a whole lot worse. So don't smoke in company.

If you're a smoker, you should acknowledge that your smoke can kill others. One day very soon, when you've given up smoking, you'll want to protect yourself against others' smoke, so, starting now, ban yourself from smoking indoors or in any other enclosed space you share with anyone, particularly your children.

Idea 31 – **Shared air**

52 Brilliant Ideas – **Quit smoking for good**

32. Team player

If you've not got the willpower to go it alone, joining a group could give you the extra resolve.

Groups might not work for everyone, but there's convincing evidence that joining and attending a specialist support group can help people overcome serious addictions to alcohol, hard drugs and gambling. Support groups also work for people who are serious about giving up cigarettes.

Quitting smoking on your own is a lonely and morale-sapping process. There's no one to confide in when your resolve starts to slip and you're wondering if it's all worth the hassle. And when you do crack and light up, there's no one around who's been there before to offer empathy or helpful strategies to get you back on track when you're full of remorse and self-loathing.

Here's an idea for you

No smoking cessation groups in your area other than ones run by idiots? Set up your own. You'll have to do some reading or pick the brains of someone running a successful group. You may also need help setting it up, with a venue and places to advertise. Plaster details and a contact number in health centres and shop windows, and arrange a preliminary meeting.

Defining idea

'Smoking is pulmonary rape.'
ANON

Groups where the focus is on overcoming a craving for nicotine will contain a cluster of individuals each with first-hand knowledge of being a smoker and each with their own insights into what does and doesn't work. When this empathy, energy, expertise and enthusiasm is pooled it's potent stuff.

Defining idea

'The believing we do something when we do nothing is the first illusion of tobacco.'
RALPH WALDO EMERSON

Non-smoking health professionals who have never given up cannot truly understand what it feels like to crave a cigarette in times of stress, but other members of the group certainly do. Some are able to put into words thoughts you feel but can't quite express, while someone else might be able to identify with a problem you talk about and suggest a useful strategy that worked for them. By taking place at prearranged intervals, group meetings also act as focal points. Thinking: 'There's a meeting on Wednesday . . . if I can just hang on' might just give you the extra impetus to keep saying no.

33. I want it now

Ever wondered why sound health and monetary gain aren't reason enough for some of us to quit?

It doesn't take long to work out how many thousands you hand over every year to your friendly tobacconist for the privilege of damaging your health. The question is, why isn't this enough to stop you smoking? Indeed, the more sensible people tell you the benefits of stopping, the more it seems to make you want to continue. Why?

The short answer is they are on the wrong wavelength. They are mixing up long- and short-term gratification. A puff of a cigarette provides a nicotine rush that hits your brain within seven seconds. These magical moments pass quickly and the heady buzz is soon replaced by a craving for more, and you know what to do about that. Saving up for that beautiful sports car, on the other hand, takes years.

Here's an idea for you

Work out how much you spend on cigarettes per day or week. Now price luxury items using these units. If a CD, say, costs three days' smoking, buy yourself one after three days; if it's a bottle of vintage champagne, buy one after a week. Make a wish list of luxuries that are currently out of your price range: that sports motorbike, designer suit, hot tub – the sky's the limit.

Defining idea

'What a weird thing smoking is ... I have a sense of wellbeing when I'm smoking, poisoning myself, killing myself slowly. ... But when I don't smoke I scarcely feel as if I'm living. I don't feel I'm living unless I'm killing myself.'
RUSSELL HOBAN

You *can* get long-term gratification from giving up smoking, but it takes time. The thing to do is get to your goal in a series of steps. The initial steps should be close together and relatively easy to achieve, then as you progress the distance between them should gradually increase. Start by rewarding yourself with small treats on a daily basis for the first week and thereafter you give yourself bigger treats less often.

It doesn't matter what you do as long as you spend all the money you would have spent on cigarettes and you spend it on the days specified. The hard bit is telling your family that all the money you'll be saving from not smoking will initially be spent on luxuries for you. If you're given a hard time, just blame us.

34. Being the help

If you're the one helping a mate to quit, here are some suggestions for you to take on board.

So you've been asked or have agreed to help a friend give up smoking. You might be wondering how you can do this, whether you are the right person to help or whether you'll just make things worse. While you can't know for sure, initial groundwork should give you some idea of your friend's motivation, what it is they need, and whether you have the necessary time and desire to help them.

Even if you have known your friend for years, we suggest that you still make a formal contract. Decide what both parties expect from the relationship, agree some basic rules and make contingency plans in case of relapses or other crises. Prearrange review dates to monitor progress. This early meeting is crucial as it can prevent a great deal of misunderstanding later on.

Here's an idea for you

You might not know how to respond to a non-specific plea for help, so be proactive. Ask your friend to text you regularly each week to catch up with how the quitting is going. If people normally buy duty-free tobacco for them when returning from holiday, draw up a list of alternatives, like perfumes, aftershave or alcohol.

Defining idea

'Teamwork makes the impossible simple.'
ANON

You might know your smoker well, but it's still worth taking a formal inventory of their smoking habit. Prepare a crib sheet of questions, and make sure they are open ones, like: What are all the different cigarettes you have each day? What will you miss about smoking? Where or when will you be most tempted to light up? What other problems do you anticipate? Have you tried to give up before and, if so, what happened (other than that you failed)? Can you imagine being a non-smoker and, if so, what would that be like?

Defining idea

'Few things are harder to put up with than the annoyance of a good example.'
MARK TWAIN

Armed with this information, you are well placed to help identify the best ways of helping your friend to quit. Some people need personal support – constant chivvying, cajoling or stroking – while others need help with organising a strategy or identifying things and places they should avoid to reduce temptation. If you have given up yourself, just being there and proving that it is possible should be a great help.

35. Ashes to ashes

It's a dirty habit. Cleaning up your act will cut down on the housework and say goodbye to airspray abuse.

Tobacco smoke has one of those pervasive odours that you can mask but never fully hide. Pump as much of that ozone-eating spring-fresh flowery 'freshener' as you like into the air and you'll still only achieve a layer of chemical gunk sitting on top of your poison cloud. It doesn't work. Cut down on the cigarette smoke and save yourself a fortune in airspray.

Stop to consider the wilful smoke damage, not to mention the threat of fire, you knowingly volunteer for every day of your life by smoking in your house. The answer is to practise damage limitation. If you can't do cold turkey, you don't need to start a complete revolution – just advance slowly. Smoke is your enemy and it's taken over your house. Drive it out, pushing the frontline ever forward.

Here's an idea for you

One by one, self-impose smoking bans on other places you smoke. Advance slowly but surely so that you ban smoking progressively throughout the house, the car, your workplace etc. When you finally have your habit cornered, go for the jugular and stop.

Defining idea

'Smoking is a custom so loathsome to the eye, hateful to the nose, harmful to the brain, dangerous to the lungs, and in the black, stinking fume thereof nearest resembling the horrible Stygian smoke of the pit that is bottomless.'
JAMES I OF ENGLAND, A Counterblaste to Tobacco

Begin by banning yourself from smoking in certain rooms. The bedroom would be a good place to start on safety grounds. Smoking and food have never been great bedfellows so rediscover the delicious aromas of cooking and ban smoking in the kitchen.

The living room might be your final frontier. It's possibly the place where you most enjoy your cigarettes, relaxing in front of the TV. So now's the time to start watching more commercial television – adverts are tailor-made for a cigarette break – and for DVDs and videos there's the pause button.

Head for the great outdoors to savour your cigarette. Once you're outside – no smoking inside any more – not only will you be giving your dwelling the chance to refresh itself, you'll also be relieving your loved ones of the chance to die young by removing the risks of passive smoking.

36. Join *them*

The rest of the world is ganging up on smokers. Maybe it's time to throw in the towel and join the majority.

Remember when the majority of adults smoked and it was possible to smoke almost anywhere? But times, they are a-changing. Now, most adults don't smoke and this majority are increasingly ensuring that the environment is kept smoke free. The no-smoking writing is on the wall everywhere. England was the latest country to outlaw smoking in public places, joining the rest of the UK, Ireland, Italy, Australia and even Cuba and Iran.

For diehard smokers, these restrictions and regulations feel like a huge intrusion on personal liberties. But when you're giving up, a ban can be a blessing. Knowing you can't light up can defer temptation. Also, being out of sight of other smokers lessens cravings. And the longer this goes on, the more you realise that perhaps you're not so badly hooked as you once thought.

Here's an idea for you

If you haven't already, make your home a no-smoking citadel. Post a 'No Smoking' plaque in a prominent place near the front entrance and, if questioned, tell visitors that you are keeping the smoking equivalent of an alcohol dry house.

Defining idea

'There are some circles in America where it seems to be more socially acceptable to carry a hand-gun than a packet of cigarettes.'
KATHARINE WHITEHORN, British journalist

There are many reasons for this hardening of attitudes: effects of passive smoking on the health of children and everyone else, the desire to prevent cigarette burns on expensive furniture and floors, and the desire to keep the air as sweet as nature had intended are just three examples that spring to mind.

Even without legal bans and domestic by-laws, the tide is turning. Today's smokers can expect a frosty reception from increasingly unpassive non-smokers and even worse from ex-addicts, some of whom have replaced their nicotine fug with an air of smugness. The once cool image of cigarettes now seems tarnished, especially amongst professionals and in middle-class circles. It still has a grip on many, but there are fewer and fewer each year. Whether tobacco will become as unfashionable as opium and be replaced by something else only time will tell.

37. Spread the word

Become a single-issue bore; make non-smoking zeal your new addiction. It could be your salvation.

You've tried patches, gone cold turkey, chewed the gum (all flavours), been counselled, seen a hypnotist, everything, and you still can't stop. Maybe, just maybe, it's time to do the one thing you thought you'd never stoop to – become a non-smoking bore. In essence, you trade in smoking for pomposity and smugness. It's a difficult one-way path with no return, but many anti-smoking gurus have happily gone there before.

Converts to the church of non-smoking are advised to start modestly – perhaps barely audible tut-tuts in the presence of a person with a lit king-size. After a week or two, start wafting smoke in a histrionic fashion to induce maximum guilt in smokers. As your confidence increases you can start to glare at smokers and mutter

Here's an idea for you

Bone up on all the famous people who've died of a smoking-related disease and use every opportunity to drop this knowledge into conversations. For instance, if someone is droning on about the wonders of psychoanalysis, you would drop in that Sigmund Freud died of cancer of the jaw.

> ### Defining idea
>
> 'People talk about 'giving up' [cigarettes] but you're not giving up anything.'
>
> **JACKIE KNOWLES, reformed smoker**

about passive smoking. (You'll need to bone up on this because it's the church's strongest weapon and needs to be cited at every available opportunity.)

When you hit your stride, these comments can be amplified into mini-lectures. The cost of cigarettes is a good one: 'Did you know that if you hadn't smoked ten a day for twenty years you'd have saved enough to buy a small sports car? Twenty a day for twenty years would get you something bigger and German.'

You know you've arrived when you can confidently boast that giving up is easy. All that stuff about addiction is rubbish, a nasty rumour started by the industry. If giving up was easy for you then it ought to be easy for lesser souls. You will now be smug, self-righteous and utterly insufferable. The people who once loved you will have long since stopped pleading with you to revert to smoking and become your former self. Instead, they'll just hate you. But you'll have the secret pleasure of knowing that your dicky heart and knackered lungs are on the mend.

38. Toothless wonder

You know smoke stains your teeth. Did you know that smoking also makes your gums rot and your teeth fall out?

Your dental hygienist could change the whole way you think about your mouth. My hygienist even taught me a whole new way to clean my teeth. I thought, foolishly, that having done it for several decades I'd mastered the art of teeth cleaning, but oh no.

I'd smoked for over 30 years and thereby affected the bones of my jaw. As a consequence my gums were severely receded. This is known as periodontal disease and it meant that my teeth were losing the support they needed to stay in place – much like you watch a sandcastle being washed away and undermined by the incoming tide. As a result, deep pockets have formed at the base of my teeth, and in these spaces bacteria have been free to have their evil way. This has further undermined the gums.

Here's an idea for you

Invest in a good anti-bacterial mouthwash, not just to improve your breath but also to flush out any bacterial pockets between your teeth. Periodontal diseases can never be cured but they can be slowed or stopped.

Defining idea

'I would not put a thief in my mouth to steal my brains.'
CHARLES PORTIS, True Grit

'Giving up smoking is the single most important thing you can do to save your teeth and gums,' is the advice. You're five times more likely to lose your teeth if you smoke, because the reduced oxygen in your bloodstream restricts the gums' ability to resist the onslaught.

To fight back, while working on giving up the weed, buy yourself a really good toothbrush. Make it an electric one because their brushing speed means that they clean more thoroughly than a hand-held brush. And don't go for the cheap option. Which brings us to toothpaste. Leave those two-for-the-price-of-one deals on the shelf: it's got to be the real thing. Go for a recognised brand that's got an anti-bacterial ingredient to help combat plaque (the film of bacteria that causes periodontal gum disease).

And that's not all you can do. Floss. Flossing brushes come in a whole range of sizes to fit between your teeth (the closer the fit the better). They can get down deep between the teeth and clear away the bacteria from those deep pockets that your regular toothbrush just won't reach. You should use these twice a day.

39. Sex or a smoke?

Would you rather give up sex or cigarettes? Sooner or later smoking is likely to win, whether you like it or not!

There are implications here for both men and women. With women, smoking has been shown to damage or destroy eggs, disrupt ovulation, screw up the menstrual cycle – particularly in middle age – and increase the risk of cancer of the cervix. Women who smoke are between two and three times less likely to get pregnant than those who don't.

Smoking when pregnant can cause damage to the unborn foetus, increase the probability of miscarriage, provoke premature birth and cause low birth weight. Women smokers hit the menopause up to four years earlier than their non-smoking sisters. They also suffer more hot flushes and are at an increased risk of heart disease and osteoporosis.

Here's an idea for you

With all the money you'll have saved after quitting, take your partner to a sex shop and buy yourselves a treat you can try out when you get home. With more energy at your disposal, as well as longer and harder erections, there's all kind of fun things you'll be able to do.

Defining idea

'Remember, if you smoke after sex you're doing it too fast.'
WOODY ALLEN

A man's penis becomes erect when aroused because it fills with blood – it has no bones or muscles. Smoking causes a build up of fatty blockages in the small arteries that lead into the penis. The result? Less blood flows in, so the erection is smaller and less hard. If your penis can't hold in the blood you'd better be quick because your erection will be here and gone before you can do much with it. Plus the fertility of your sperm can drop by over 50%, and the reduced testosterone diminishes your sex drive, which means you won't be capable of having sex as often.

Defining idea

'In the UK, about 120,000 men in their 30s and 40s are needlessly impotent because of smoking.'
COMIC COMPANY, 'Sex and Smoking' leaflet

So ask yourself, is it worth it? Cutting down on cigarettes is clearly going to help but cutting them out altogether has got to be the ultimate answer. You can use sexual pleasure as a tool to achieve this end.

40. Older and wiser

With the benefit of hindsight, think about just what lessons you would be able to teach your pre-smoking self.

Young you: *You smoke, don't you: why do you carry on?* **Old you:** Yes, but I wish I'd never started. I can't stop. It's a drug addiction. *Lots of people give up drugs, it can't be that hard.* You don't know what it's like, and I hope you never do. *Surely it's just willpower?* Everyone fools themselves that one can't hurt; that they're strong enough to quit any time they want. Except they never quite get round to it – and then they die.

How did you get started? It seemed a grown-up thing to do. Smoking looked cool. *Did you enjoy it?* I felt sick and dizzy the first time I tried it. But lots of my friends smoked and I didn't want to be left out, so I stuck at it until I could smoke without coughing my lungs up. *You've always got a cough nowadays and you sound dreadful in the morning.*

Here's an idea for you

Buddy up with a fellow smoker and quit together. Support each other with ideas and tips. Always be on the end of a phone for one another. Ring up when you desperately want a smoke and talk each other out of it.

Defining idea

'I knew what they were doing to injure people, to get children addicted to this product so they have another customer for 10, 15, 20 years. Believe me, fighting this doesn't make you a hero. It makes you a human being.'

PATRICIA HENLEY, successful judgement against tobacco companies in Los Angeles courts, 2005

How different would your life have been if you hadn't started smoking? I know I'll die ten years earlier than I need to – if I'm lucky. I'll leave my family stranded. I'd have been healthier, without any doubt, and I'd have had a lot more money to do things with – I could almost have bought a house with the money I've wasted on the weed.

So, you've got nothing good to say about smoking? Absolutely not. If I had my time again I'd never have lit that first cigarette. *That first cigarette was hard to smoke, and I'm sure the last one will be even harder. But listening to yourself, you'll know quitting's the right thing to do. You owe it to everyone to stop now; it's never too late.*

41. Staying alive

If you die early or become disabled through smoking you're not the only victim. Think of your family.

How about you? How important is it to you that you're around for your children as they grow up into adults? As smokers, can we be sure that we'll be there? And do you want them to have to look after an invalid in your declining years? What about your partner – how will they feel struggling with someone unable to do anything for themselves and then being abandoned to struggle through retirement alone?

There are two issues here: you and your children. Your child will plead, 'Please don't smoke any more.' It's not only because they've been educated in school about the evils of smoking. It's also because they can see with their own eyes that you cough your lungs up every morning; that you can't play football any more, or run up hills with them like you used to. And they love you to join in.

Here's an idea for you

Imagine you have been given the gift of an extra five or ten years of life. Write down all the things you'd like to do with that extra time – and give yourself at least two thousand a year extra as spending money. Stop smoking tomorrow and your dream may come true.

Defining idea

'R.J. Reynolds has a long history of working to reduce the risks associated with smoking cigarettes. Smoking is addictive. The best way to reduce the risks of smoking, of course, is to quit.'
R.J. REYNOLDS INDUSTRIES WEBSITE, 2005

It's also about you. You're an adult and you've lived long enough to be able to have a concept of the future. We really ought to know better because we know where our path is leading. Don't you want to be there for your child's wedding? Do you really want to watch your grandchildren play from your wheelchair, grunting as you reach for your portable nebuliser or draw your blanket up round the stumps of your legs?

We all need to grow up and realise our responsibilities as spouses and parents. They don't end when your child leaves home; they continue until the day you die. Why die early or in agony, and deny them and you all those additional years of pleasure? Carry on smoking and you're just being selfish.

Idea 41 – **Staying alive**

52 Brilliant Ideas – **Quit smoking for good**

42. Home sweet home

Decorating your home is a great way to celebrate and reinforce your decision to quit.

If you have been smoking inside, rather than in the garden, the legacy of your habit will be everywhere. The stink of stale tobacco will have permeated the curtains, carpets, walls and soft furnishings. A fresh lick of paint or steam cleaning the carpets are ways of actively demonstrating your commitment to a new life – a life without cigarettes. And, hopefully, having spent time, money and energy improving your property, you'll be less inclined to return it to a state of nicotine-stained squalor by smoking inside again.

During the transition period while you are quitting, it is a good idea to stay away from the temptation of places like pubs and bars where other people are puffing away. A newly decorated home will feel more welcoming and you are more likely to want to stay in.

Here's an idea for you

Synchronise the date you stop smoking with a campaign to improve your home. You can use the money you would have spent on cigarettes to buy materials and tools. Working on your home will not only improve your physical environment but also burn up nervous energy when you are fighting cravings to smoke again.

Defining idea

'If you must smoke, take your butt outside.'
ANON

We are not talking about a quick once-over with a large tin of whitewash. What we have in mind is far more radical and enjoyable. A home makeover can be a thing you do for yourself rather than something that happens to strangers on daytime TV. Most large bookshops have a varied collection of 'how to' books, brimming with suggestions about how to transform a dump into a desirable dwelling.

Before you get to the enjoyable creative bits, you have the less than thrilling task of preparatory work. Painting over nicotine-soaked ceilings and walls is only a short-term solution, because sooner rather than later the brown sludge will penetrate through the new eggshell or emulsion. Fortunately, good old sugar soap has also had a makeover and now comes in a spray-on form, making it ideal to cut through the grease and provide the perfect key for new paint. And while you are seeing the damage smoke has done to your property, it's worth considering what the same stuff, in a concentrated form, has been doing to your lungs.

43. Smash your habit

Give your ashtrays, lighters and other smoking accoutrements a death sentence. Then you've passed the point of no return.

Look around your manor and you'll see evidence of your smoking habit everywhere. We're not talking about a nicotine-stained ceiling or cigarette burns on the sideboard. Think ashtrays – be they glass ones, china ones or metal ones 'borrowed' from pubs – and lighters – iconic petrol designs, classics that double up as flame-throwers, disposable ones you have never managed to dispose of. Then there are cigarette cases, presentation boxes and tobacco tins that are now used to store stuff.

These things are a constant reminder of the hold tobacco had, and maybe continues to have, on your life. Getting rid of this motley collection is about burning your bridges and passing the point of no return. It also sends out a clear message to your family, and

Here's an idea for you

Atomising this stuff is profoundly rewarding and is a pleasure to be shared with friends and family. Get everyone to throw heavy objects at your redundant ashtrays and join in with hammering your lighters. Other families might want to contribute their own collections to keep the fun going.

Defining idea

'One thousand Americans stop smoking every day – by dying.'
ANON

especially your children, that cigarettes might have had a big part of your past but they are not going to have much of a say in your future.

When we say 'get rid of this collection' we're not talking about loading up the car and taking a trip to your local charity shop or the dump. We envisage you physically smashing the collection to bits: smashing china and glass ashtrays into three-dimensional 1000-piece jigsaws, converting tobacco tins and metal ashtrays into worthless but interestingly shaped scrap metal, and flattening lighters with a sledgehammer. This might all seem a bit severe, especially if some of this stuff was given to you as presents, but the battle against smoking is bigger than that.

The Duke of Wellington arrived at a personal crossroads when in his late teens: whether to become a musician, like his father, or turn his back on music and become a soldier. He burnt his violin. Smashing your ashtrays could be your Waterloo.

44. Trial separation

Your relationship with cigarettes is souring. You want out. But how? Time apart might be the answer.

You've got some leave booked. You want to quit, but aren't quite sure. You and cigarettes go back a long way. They've been part of your life for years, decades perhaps; always there at times of stress, disappointment or celebration. But the cough is getting worse and non-smoking colleagues on the same pay band always seem to have more money than you. Should you take your cigarettes on holiday with you or put them in kennels?

Here are some reasons for using a holiday to toy with the notion of giving up smoking. You're away from the glare of family, friends and ill-wishers. You will be away from your usual routines and triggers that make lighting up almost a reflex action. You will be removed from workplace stressors and tensions. And, if you do decide

Here's an idea for you

If you haven't got two weeks, try a mini-break from smoking by taking your nearest and dearest to the seaside, a spa town or the hills for a couple of days. Every time you feel like lighting up, take a few deep breaths of clean air and feel deservedly smug as you get the nicotine out of your system.

Defining idea

'The best way to stop smoking is to carry wet matches.'
ANON

to give up, you will have got over the initial withdrawals before returning to your old routine and work.

Get thinking about the different types of holiday. Many destinations, like Ireland and New York, have banned smoking in restaurants, bars and most public spaces. That's just what you need when you are trying to give up. If you choose a more distant destination, you'll have the additional advantage of a long (non-smoking) flight, which, added to the long (non-smoking) wait beforehand, should set you well on your way to overcoming the first hurdle – the physical addiction to nicotine – thereby freeing you up to concentrate on the psychological aspects.

There's a whole range of activity-based holidays you can enjoy without cigarettes: potholing, survival training, wind surfing, scuba diving, etc. Essentially, you get so involved in the pursuits that you'll be too knackered to even think about cigarettes during the day, and at the end of it you'll just be glad to hit the sack. Courses where physical effort is required will also improve your fitness no end.

45. Duty free

Holiday madness. Who could possibly turn down such a bargain as half-price cigarettes? You can.

When we sniff a bargain like half-price cigarettes, it's like putting on blinkers. If it looks like we're going to save money, we forget entirely how much more we'd save if we didn't buy them at all. What's half of nothing? Nothing. That's what you'll spend if you don't fall into the duty-free trap.

Holidays are supposed to be treats so why not use your money wisely instead of sending it up in smoke? Explore the local stores or the duty-free shop properly. They don't just sell cigarettes and alcohol. There are many other goods to choose from which are much cheaper without the taxes at home. Buy perfume, a digital camera, a personal stereo. Some of these will be a source of pleasure to you for years to come. A cigarette lasts only a few minutes.

Here's an idea for you

Use the airport as a portal to a smoke-free life. Vow you will not step back onto home soil as a smoker. Go two weeks without cigarettes and you'll already feel the difference. You'll also have begun to conquer the cravings, which means you won't fall into the duty-free trap.

Defining idea

'If we see you smoking we will assume you are on fire and take appropriate action.'
DOUGLAS ADAMS

Part of the pleasure of going abroad is the opportunity to explore a different way of life. Use the money you haven't spent on cigarettes to do something you've never done before. Treat yourself to something exotic. It might be something produced locally, like clothing or pottery. It could be an extra trip out, scuba diving, deep-sea fishing, or a five-star meal.

Defining idea

'Smoking is very bad for you and should only be done because it looks so good. People who don't smoke have a terrible time finding something polite to do with their lips.'
P.J. O'ROURKE, American humorist

If you saved up all the money you spend on cigarettes – both on holiday and at home – you could very easily have a substantial amount towards buying your own holiday home. More immediately, the money you'd save in a single year will go a long way towards paying for your holiday next year. Pick up a brochure and start planning now.

46. It's quiz time

Here's the question of a lifetime. Do you (a) keep smoking or (b) quit now or start on the road to giving up?

The prize in this quiz is that you'll live as long as possible and keep as much of your own money as you can. All you have to do is go through the following statements and decide whether option (a) is the way to go or if (b) is the better choice.

Your first decision here determines whether you give a lion's share of your money to the tobacco giants and the taxman or keep it yourself. (a) or (b)? Get the idea?

Given that more and more companies won't employ smokers, you can easily limit your future by keeping on smoking. Talking of limits, impotence and sterility threatens. Will you choose sex or death?

Here's an idea for you

Draw a column of smoke with notches for every pack of cigarettes you buy – like those fundraising thermometers outside schools or churches – and mark off against it what you could have bought instead of cigarettes.

Defining idea

'If you can't send money, send tobacco.'
GEORGE WASHINGTON

If you didn't smoke you could afford an extra holiday every year. But bear in mind that you have less choice of hotels to stay in if you're a smoker. Or, as a non-smoker, you could put a lot more into your pension. Shame you smoked. By now your mortgage would have been almost paid off. Plus you'll have to spend any savings to buy all the stuff you'll need once you're house-bound through smoking-related illness.

Defining idea

'I'll give you a definite maybe.'
SAMUEL GOLDWYN, movie producer

Give up smoking now and enjoy five to ten more years of life. Keep on smoking and you can give up sport, then walking and then breathing. You could also kill your family and friends through passive smoking while you smoke. Finally, your children beg you to give up. Do you choose death or your children?

If you chose (b) for all your answers, congratulations! The prize is yours. If (a) was your preferred answer, you get the booby prize. You muppet!

47. Use hate power

You've tried it all to give up but you're still puffing away. It's time to become a perverse philanthropist.

Most of us like to think that we wish all our fellow humans well. We have a relaxed attitude to organisations like single-issue pressure groups, extreme political parties, cults and religions. They are just part of life's rich tapestry. What utter bollocks! There are people whose downfall would give us immense pleasure and companies we pray might go bust.

This idea looks at a way to harness these negative feelings and use the power of hate to help you quit smoking. Identify a target who it would crucify you to give serious money to. For example, you might feel angry with a charity that exploits a sentimental love of animals to get the elderly to leave money to a donkey sanctuary. If you were robbed of your rightful

Here's an idea for you

If you're money rich and time poor, having to spend your insufficient off-duty periods doing humiliating work should you fall off the non-smoking wagon could be a great way of keeping yourself motivated. The prospect of having to spend Sunday mornings clearing litter from your local park while others languish in bed might just help keep you in line.

Defining idea

'... the main reason many Americans have for smoking heavily, is that smoking is a fairly sure, fairly honourable form of suicide.'
KURT VONNEGUT

inheritance by just such a ploy, imagine how much worse you would feel if you compounded the fury by giving the sods even more money, and money you can't afford? How's that for motivation?

Let's say you've gone for a loathsome political party who'd just love to have a donation from you. You next need to draw up a contract. For instance, 'I, John Brown, promise that if I haven't quit smoking by 24 July 2007, I will send the enclosed predated cheque for £1000 to the Young Nazi Party and ask to be added to their mailing list. Signed in the presence of . . .' Give the cheque and a covering letter to someone who promises to grass on you if you revert to smoking.

Carry a copy of this contract around with you. Read it every time you feel the urge. Fume as you visualise the pleasure your unsolicited gift would give to someone or something you intensely dislike!

48. Keep on quitting

Quitting for good might seem like climbing Everest. Break it down into stages to make the impossible possible.

To start off, list all of the reasons why you want to give up smoking. Keep the list with you and read it through before you light up. Don't deny yourself any cigarettes at this stage. Then start messing around with your usual smoking routines. If you have two smoking breaks at work, try having them both in the morning and introduce a tea-only break in the afternoon. At this stage, you don't need to focus on smoking any less, just attack your rituals. If you destabilise your habits, it's easier to break them.

Next you'll be ready to pick a quit date. Select your preferred way of quitting (there should be at least one Brilliant Idea here that appeals to you) and buy any aids you might need, like nicotine gum or dried fruit. Set yourself some specific and attainable goals. For instance, 'I want to get through

Here's an idea for you

When you relapse, it's tempting to think of it as an all-or-nothing failure. 'What the heck, I've had one, I may as well smoke the whole packet.' Nothing could be further from the truth. If you smoke one cigarette, that's all you've done, smoked a measly cigarette. Why let that defeat you? The fewer cigarettes you smoke and the sooner you think about stopping again the better. After all, practice makes perfect.

Defining idea

'Remember you did not enjoy being a smoker. That's why you stopped. You enjoy being an ex-smoker.'
ALLEN CARR, non-smoking guru

the weekend without smoking' is a realistic start and means you won't be setting yourself up to fail.

Try to make your quit date as relaxed and stress free as possible. You might like to have a day off and be pampered at a health farm, or you may prefer to throw yourself into work and distract yourself from smoking as much as possible. Whatever you decide, it's vital that you throw away all your cigarettes. No ifs and buts. You've passed the point of no return.

After you've done the hard bit, you've got to stay strong and stay motivated. Remember why you gave up in the first place and keep changing your routine to avoid those smoking triggers. Above all, feel pride in what you've achieved so far.

49. Idle hands

With time on your hands, the addict inside you will be begging for one last cigarette. Stay active.

With smoking out of your life, it's important to see the extra time saved as a gift rather than a burden. The extra years of life you'll gain are easier to deal with because you can plan larger projects. With the extra money you'll save there are opportunities for holidays, redesigning the garden or choosing interesting courses to go on.

The more challenging aspect of extra time is on a day-to-day basis: all those five minutes not spent smoking. If you take cigarette breaks at work, the chances are you'll be hanging out with the smokers behind the bike sheds (or wherever you've been banished to). Not having to do that any more can give you a chance to meet new people and mingle with the non-smokers. Then there are all those novels you could read, slotting chapters into the odd five minutes here and there. You could even rediscover the art of letter writing and pen some lines to long-lost friends.

Here's an idea for you

Celebrate the new you with a calendar of fresh ideas. Draw up a list of 52 new things to do in the coming year, one for each week.

Defining idea

'I kissed my first girl and smoked my first cigarette on the same day. I haven't had time for tobacco since.'
ARTURO TOSCANINI

Food is a great replacement for cigarettes – though not just any old food, unless you want to look like the Michelin Man. With your taste buds returning to normal you'll be able to relish the pleasure of fine food, but you will need to keep a weather eye on the calorie content. Smokeless and fat free is the new you. Fresh fruit and vegetables (you need five portions a day anyway) are great for experimenting with. You can prepare them in advance and carry them in a snack box to dip into whenever you fancy. Herbal and fruit teas (without sugar) can also help your palate to explore your new sense of taste.

Make the extra time work for you. Expanding your interests and taking on new challenges will help to break up the patterns of the old, smoking you. Be novel and adventurous. Just don't waste it by giving in to the cravings.

50. Stay stopped

Nicotine will always be waiting to ambush you, so train yourself to become an instinctive non-smoker.

You're a smoker, even when you've stopped – just a smoker who happens not to smoke any more. So every day you'll have to face not having that first cigarette. Those deeply ingrained paths still exist inside you and the Tobacco Demon never completely goes away.

Life is made up of patterns, and humans love to tread those comforting, familiar paths. Smoking is one such ritual, each cigarette a little cycle of actions we grow accustomed to. What you must do more than anything is disrupt those routines that trigger the desire to smoke. Change the ways you do things, especially anything that you can connect to smoking – where you sit, how you use the telephone, what order you do things in. Break up the smoking pattern and create a new non-smoking one in its place.

Here's an idea for you

Analyse your habit. Write a list of when you smoke and why. Tackle each one as an individual challenge. Remember you're a smoker who really wants to stop and remind yourself why quitting is such a good idea.

Defining idea

'I'll go to a club [in Britain], but you guys smoke so friggin' much, I can't sing for ages after. If everyone in England stops smoking cigarettes then I'll come and party.'
MARIAH CAREY, singer

Support is a vital ingredient in the recipe for success. In particular, members of your family can provide the extra discipline and morale boosts to keep you on the straight and narrow. Having others to encourage you will make a big difference to your chances of packing in for good. They'll want you to quit and be proud of you when you do.

There's a terrible sense of defeat about continuing smoking even though you know you want to stop. Your sense of self-esteem is rock bottom. The good thing is that the opposite is true when you do stop. You'll feel great and glow with the sense of achievement. Believe in yourself. You are stronger than your addiction. You're not going to be fooled any more, be a slave to the profiteering giants of the tobacco industry, or fill the government's pockets with any more wasted money.

51. One can't hurt?

One cigarette isn't just one – it's the first of many. As soon as you light up you're back on the old treadmill.

It's said one thing leads to another. For smokers never a truer word was spoken. Why settle for one when you can have two? The first one or two you'll cadge off friends, smokers who are more than happy to have you rejoin the fold. Then you'll find yourself wanting some of your own. But you'll be good; you'll only buy a packet of ten. You'll set limits, fooling yourself that this time you'll control the habit, not the other way around. You'll manage on two a day.

And two will become five, and five will become ten. You'll have lots of good reasons why it's okay. Besides, tomorrow you'll go back to two. And, of course, you can quit any time you want. But you never do. Then the day will come (and it won't take long) when you buy that first packet of twenty. By then, believe me, you're a smoker again. And all because of one cigarette.

Here's an idea for you

Starting today, become a collector and save up all your dog ends (carry a handy bag to pop them into). Find some see-through plastic containers to display your collection in a prominent place. That'll show you what you've been up to.

Defining idea

'[The tobacco companies] are, in effect, mass killers.
They are committing genocide by their products.'

JOHN CRONIN, British MP and consultant surgeon

At this stage, you'll have to go through the whole process of stopping again, and you won't be in the best shape to do it. You'll feel defeated, disappointed in yourself, a failure. If you're not careful you can convince yourself that this proves it: you'll never be able to give up, so why fight it?

That's the Tobacco Demon in you talking. When wake up one day and feel angry with yourself for caving in and decide to give it another go, the Demon will agree with you. At the same time he'll point out that you've still got most of a pack left, so why not smoke those while you're setting up your next attempt? Tomorrow will do just as well as today. Stop fooling yourself. Do it now; quit again today. And don't reach for just one more cigarette while you muster your resolve.

52. Dog ends

Mark each day you don't smoke as it takes you further towards reclaiming your life and your health.

Celebrate. You've stopped; you're an ex-smoker. Quite apart from the fact that you're richer, you also don't smell as bad, you're more employable (lots of companies don't like smokers), your food tastes better and your sense of smell has improved, your self-esteem is on a high, the chances of your loved ones suffering from passive smoking drop dramatically and, last but not least, there's your improved health. Here are your milestones of success.

- Twenty minutes after smoking your last cigarette your heart rate drops and twelve hours later the carbon monoxide level in your blood drops to normal.
- Three months after quitting, the risk of you suffering a heart attack begins to drop. Your lung function begins to improve.

Here's an idea for you

Still smoking? Choose a wall in your house or flat and paint it white. Buy a permanent marker pen. For every cigarette you smoke, draw a dot on the wall. See how long it takes to turn the wall completely black. Then it will match your lungs.

Defining idea

'They know they're selling death now. They're not stupid. They just don't choose to admit it.'
SIR GEORGE GODBER, UK Chief Medical Officer for Health, 1960–72

- Nine months after quitting, your coughing and shortness of breath decrease.
- One year after quitting, your added risk of coronary heart disease is half that of a smoker's, and after five years your stroke risk is reduced to that of a non-smoker's.

Any recovering drug addict feels stressed. What you don't need to do is head back into the same old habits to relieve the stress. If you stick with your non-smoking lifestyle, you could wipe the slate clean in ten to fifteen years.

Brilliant ideas

This book is published by Infinite Ideas, creators of the acclaimed **52 Brilliant Ideas** series. If you found this book helpful, there are other titles in the **Brilliant Little Ideas** series which you may also find of interest.

- **Be incredibly creative**
- **Catwalk looks**
- **Drop a dress size**
- **Enjoy great sleep**
- **Find your dream job**
- **Get fit!**
- **Heal your troubled mind**
- **Healthy children's lunches**
- **Incredible sex**
- **Make your money work**
- **Perfect romance**
- **Quit smoking for good**
- **Raising young children**
- **Relax**
- **Seduce anyone**
- **Shape up your bum**
- **Shape up your life**

For more detailed information on these books and others published by Infinite Ideas please visit www.infideas.com.

See reverse for order form.

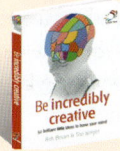

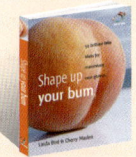

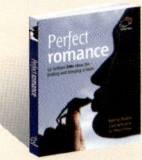

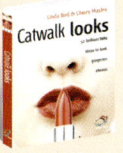

52 Brilliant Ideas – **Quit smoking for good**

Qty	Title	RRP
	Be incredibly creative	£5.99
	Catwalk looks	£5.99
	Drop a dress size	£5.99
	Enjoy great sleep	£5.99
	Find your dream job	£5.99
	Get fit!	£5.99
	Heal your troubled mind	£5.99
	Healthy children's lunches	£5.99
	Incredible sex	£5.99
	Make your money work	£5.99
	Perfect romance	£5.99
	Quit smoking for good	£4.99
	Raising young children	£5.99
	Relax	£5.99
	Seduce anyone	£5.99
	Shape up your bum	£5.99
	Shape up your life	£5.99

Add £2.49 postage per delivery address

Final TOTAL

Name: ....

Delivery address: ....

....

....

E-mail:..........................Tel (in case of problems):

By post Fill in all relevant details, cut out or copy this page and send along with a cheque made payable to Infinite Ideas. Send to: Brilliant Little Ideas, Infinite Ideas, 36 St Giles, Oxford OX1 3LD. **Credit card orders over the telephone** Call +44 (0) 1865 514 888. Lines are open 9am to 5pm Monday to Friday.

Please note that no payment will be processed until your order has been dispatched. Goods are dispatched through Royal Mail within 14 working days, when in stock. We never forward personal details on to third parties or bombard you with junk mail. The prices quoted are for UK and RoI residents only. If you are outside these areas please contact us for postage and packing rates. Any questions or comments please contact us on 01865 514 888 or email info@infideas.com.